FROM COUNTRY BOY
TO WEATHERMAN
A HOUGHTON AND DUNSTABLE YOUTH

George Jackson

The
Book
Castle

First published November 2006 by
The Book Castle
12 Church Street
Dunstable
Bedfordshire LU5 4RU

ISBN 1 903747 81 3
ISBN   978 1 903747 81 0

Designed and typeset by Tracey Moren
Moren Associates Limited
www.morenassociates.co.uk

Printed in Great Britain by Cromwell Press, Trowbridge, Wiltshire

CONTENTS

ACKNOWLEDGEMENTS

Two earlier Book Castle publications – Old Houghton Including Upper Houghton by Pat Lovering and Dunstable School 1888 – 1971 by F M Bancroft – have greatly assisted my fading memory and I am grateful to their authors for that help. My friend, John Hall, provided a treasure trove of archive material about the Meteorological Office years, including several letters to him that I had forgotten even writing. This made my task much easier and I offer John my sincere thanks. My sister, Jennifer Rayner, helped with putting names to familiar faces – a skill I sometimes lack!

Sally Siddons, of The Book Castle, has kindly and very gently guided me through the processes leading to publication and her help has been invaluable. My deepest thanks, however, must go to my wife Haidee for putting up for so long with a husband often oblivious to everything except the work in progress.

INTRODUCTION AND DEDICATION

B oth my grandmother and my mother and to a lesser extent my father had a great fund of stories from the past that we as children loved to hear, as they really brought that past to life for us. 'Tell us a story' was a plea we often made to Gran Maud to pass away a rainy day or to delay the inevitable bedtime. In later years, when we got back from the pub, it would be Mum and Dad who entertained us with their recollections over a supper of cheese and Branston brown sauce sandwiches. Sadly there seems little time for storytelling nowadays, but hopefully this written miscellany of memories from the first part of my life will serve as my version of that story telling tradition and be enjoyed in the same way. This book is therefore dedicated to those whose memory inspired me to write it:

Maud Humphrey	1896 - 1974
George W Jackson	1910 - 2000
Betty Jackson	1916 - 2002

George W H Jackson
Thornbury, South Gloucestershire
2006

ABOUT THE AUTHOR

George W H Jackson was born in Houghton Regis in 1941, the eldest of four children. He attended Whitehead C of E Primary School in the village and then Dunstable Grammar School. His first job was as a Scientific Assistant for the Meteorological Office in various departments at Dunstable, at RAF Bovingdon and subsequently at Bracknell in Berkshire.

He joined the Huntingdonshire Constabulary, (later Mid-Anglia and now Cambridgeshire), serving at Huntingdon, St Ives and Sawtry before transferring to the Pembrokeshire Division of the Dyfed Powys Constabulary. On leaving the police, he worked for a period with the Herald Bard of Wales before becoming Landlord of the Brook Inn at St Ishmaels in Pembrokeshire.

Towards the end of his six years in the licensed trade he became part-time Clerk & Financial Officer to Pembroke Town Council before being appointed Town Clerk at  Thornbury in South Gloucestershire in 1984. Since early retirement, he has been involved in community transport provision and has also served as President of the Hearts of Oak Friendly Society.

George is married to Haidee and they have two adult sons, Bill and Douglas. His interests include cricket, now watching rather than playing, and ideally in warmer climates than ours.

1

IN THE BEGINNING

I was born in Houghton Regis, Bedfordshire on 9th May 1941 when I was several weeks premature – not that you would guess that fact now with my height just on six feet and a weight that would give me a perfect body mass index if I was seven feet five. My mother described me at birth as looking like a skinned rabbit without a bum, and my great grandmother Lizzie Humphrey, having been pushed up from the village in a wheelchair to see the new arrival, made the fortunately incorrect pronouncement, 'take me home - it'll never thrive.'

Still no bum, but obviously thriving despite Granny Lizzie's gloomy forecast

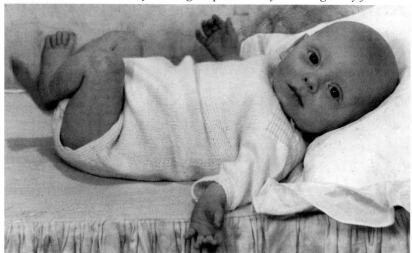

Mum and Dad had married in 1939 and I was their first-born. Two sisters, one brother and ten years after me, they decided that four was enough or as my brother Nigel would tell you they thought they couldn't improve on perfection! Mother was a local girl but father was a Brummie, having come to the area when AC-Sphinx (later AC-Delco, a division of General Motors) moved their main factory from Birmingham to Dunstable. Not long after the move Dad met mother and soon became his future mother-in-law's lodger. The rest, as they say, is history.

George and his bride Betty had a new house built on a small field off Sundon Road known as Hyde Park, which was then very much on the outskirts of the village. Their home was built by a local builder called Newell, cost just over £800 and they moved in after their wedding, which was on 10th April. This house, 'The Hyde', was where I spent all of my childhood, most of my teenage years and regular happy visits until the 1970s when my father took retirement a year early. The house was then sold to the same council that had tried to purchase it compulsorily some years earlier and failed when my parents won an appeal at a public inquiry. The vegetable garden and orchard were built on first, but the council put tenants in the house for a number of years before it was finally demolished. I helped my parents move out and often wondered what the new occupants had thought when they went into the kitchen and discovered that I had been busy on the walls with a felt tipped pen, drawing a kitchen cupboard where the kitchen cupboard used to be, a table where the table used to be and a clock where the clock used to be showing the time when Mum and Dad had walked out for the last time.

Pre-school memories are dim but happy. We always had

The Hyde, Sundon Road – my birthplace and home of many memories

chickens and often other types of poultry and I remember feeding and spending time with the chickens and giving them all names – most were after my relatives. The large hen that seemed to take charge of all the others was definitely Gran Maud, the slimmer one who ran around a lot was Aunty Rose and the smart, jaunty cockerel was Uncle Joe. We only had one cockerel so Uncle Ron was actually female! My mother was an only child and at this time my father was estranged from his family, so my aunts and uncles were actually of the great variety – my grandmother's three sisters

3

and their husbands and they really were great in their different ways.

Aunt Alice was Gran Maud's half-sister and considerably older. She and her husband George Hunt also lived in Houghton Regis in the same terrace of cottages in Bedford Road as my grandmother who lived with her mother Lizzie Humphrey. Alice and George both died when I was still quite young and memories are somewhat limited, but I do remember a sweetie jar and a glass case full of stuffed ducks, which were taken out for me to play with if I was good. For some reason, Alice always referred to her husband as 'Brother Hunt' and he always called her 'Tarney'. Aunty Gert was married to George Germaine (always known to the family as Geo or Joe). They had a house in St Michaels Avenue, which again was only a few yards from Maud and Lizzie. Very early memories are of special birthday and Christmas presents and Uncle Joe's unusual but quite pleasant smell when you sat on his lap, which later in life I discovered to be a mixture of nicotine and best bitter! – they came into their own later in my life. Aunty Rose and her husband Ron Thomson lived a few miles away in Winfield Street, Dunstable, and it was with Rose that I had most contact, as she visited almost every weekday by bus, always with sweets or biscuits wrapped in a multitude of brown paper bags in the depths of her shopping bag which in later years contained comics and money – also wrapped in brown paper bags so that 'He' wouldn't know how much she had got. Strangely, none of the three sisters had any children so, often to the consternation of Mum, we were frequently 'spoiled'.

One particular pre-school memory involves Aunty Rose. I had been ill – no idea what with and she decided some air would do me good. She borrowed a wheelchair, or even a bath chair, from

*Four generations – Grannie Lizzie Humphrey, Gran Maud and Mum pose
with the first of the next generation*

somewhere in the village, pushed it empty all the way to our house, loaded me up complete with blankets and set off up Sundon Road, which was then little more than a country lane, for a 'good walk'. But Rose being Rose, there were frequent stops to delve into the brown paper bags and to pick wild flowers which were made into a bouquet for Mum and used to decorate the wheelchair, so much so that I came back feeling like the King of the May but probably looking more like the Queen! I don't remember being a particularly sickly child but I do remember having to have a vapour lamp by my bedside and having my chest rubbed with Vick and various other concoctions because I suffered from croup. I also remember thinking, probably because of the sound of the word, that I must have caught croup from the chickens.

Going back to chickens, I am told and I think I have a faint memory of it, that at a very early age I became a hen murderer. One of our chickens went missing one day and, after fruitless searching, Dad decided that the foxes must have had it. Some time later he found the long-dead fowl inside an old cast iron boiler that had once been used to cook up their feed of bran and potato peelings. Questioned, I remembered that I had been playing with the chickens as usual, decided to pretend to cook one and that it had gone 'kwyrrrrrrk' when I put the lid on!

Soon after my mother and father moved into 'The Hyde' they were told that as they had spare accommodation they must accept servicemen being billeted with them as compulsory lodgers – a great way to start married life. So a succession of strangers, mostly airmen from a small installation nearby, shared our home one or two at a time for a number of years. Some of them my mother remembered quite fondly but others much less so. I remember only

one, an American, one of mother's favourites, who used to call me 'Punkin'. I had no idea then that he was an American and no idea then or now what Punkin means (little punk presumably?) but I did know and still remember that he seemed to have a never-ending supply of chocolate on the top shelf in his wardrobe and was quite happy to let me have some on a very regular basis. Many years later, on my first visit to America, I immediately recognised Hershey Bars as my personal wartime aid from the States.

My only other wartime memory is of being at a Christmas party at a big house in the village and bursting into tears when Father Christmas appeared. A lady in uniform comforted me – I'm told it was a pretty, young WAAF and I spent the rest of the party sitting on her lap enjoying a cuddle. Apparently I was very reluctant to leave my new friend when the party ended and I honestly remember really enjoying the experience – shades of later life perhaps?

My first experience of death, human rather than chicken, came before I was five when my great grandmother Lizzie died. Apparently she got up later and later each day until one day she didn't get up at all and then just very gently faded away, quite a nice way to go. My memory is of coming home from Lizzie's house sitting on the little saddle fixed to the crossbar of Dad's bike and him saying in a rather strange voice that, 'she hadn't been a bad old stick.' I wasn't allowed to go to the funeral, someone stayed to look after me and I remember feeling a bit left out and curious as to what I may have missed. Hopefully, Lizzie was insured because in terms of weekly family income the funeral didn't come cheap. The 2nd February 1946 bill from Edgar Franklin, Undertaker & Funeral Director of Church Street, Dunstable, reads:

To making Waxed Polished Brass
Furnished Elm Coffin Fitted with Robe,
Swans Satin Side Sheets, Frilled and
Lined complete.

Provided and Paid Bearers & all
Gratuities to Drivers, Grave Digger. etc.
etc.

Provided Saloon Motor Hearse & Paid
Fees for Single Depth Grave at Houghton
Regis & Minister's Fees complete.   14 10 0

A/c for Wreaths & Acknowledgements
in Local Press   10 6

                                              £15 0 6d

The bill was paid in full two days later.

My only other very early memory is of the VE celebration party held on The Green. One photograph shows me sitting at the head of one of the long rows of trestle tables and clearly much more interested in what was on my plate than the photographer or anything else that was going on. All I remember about the event is having types of cake different to those that Mum made and having several different colour jellies on the same dish. Obviously food

V.E. Day celebrations on The Green
I am far-left in the fawn coat with the trendy velvet collar

has always been important to me.

2

THE SCHOOL ON THE GREEN

There were two schools in the village – the County Primary, which was always known as 'Top School' by virtue of its location at one end of the village rather than by any particular sort of merit, and the Charity Endowed Voluntary Primary, which was known sometimes as 'Bottom School', more often as 'The School on the Green', and later evolved into the Whitehead Church of England Primary. At the age of five I was sent to the school on the green. It couldn't have made much of an initial impression, as, when Mum collected me at the end of my first day and asked how I had got on, I apparently said, 'it was alright but I don't think I'll bother going tomorrow.' My first teacher was Miss Freeman who seemed to be incredibly old and probably was fairly advanced in years, as she had also taught my mother and my grandmother who both mystified me at the time by always referring to Miss Freeman, who was pencil slim, as 'Lardy'. I discovered later that 'Lardy' was actually a contraction of Lah-di-dah because she was a bit prim and proper and very well spoken. This she was but she was also very kind and understanding of us first-timers as she showed when one lad, not realising you could ask to go or too frightened to speak, wet his trousers in the middle of a lesson.

In Miss Freeman's class we learned to write and do sums not

with paper and pen or pencil but with slates and chalk. We each had slates about nine inches by fifteen inches in a wooden frame. The slates were double sided with one side being plain and the other having permanent horizontal lines marked on it. The plain side was for drawing and sums and the lined side was for writing. Another teaching aid in the infant class was a strip of leather with a line of eyelets and laces to practice lacing and tying bows. By the time we had finished we could do laces in three different patterns and tie both single and double bows – useful for lacing up and tying shoes or even the boots that a few of the lads wore.

Eventually we moved on from the slates to pencils and pens. Pencils were only for drawing, but for all writing and for sums pens had to be used. The pens were wooden 'dip' pens with steel nibs filled from inkwells fitted into our desks and capable of delivering enormous blots if not used with care. Blotting paper and new nibs were obviously in short supply, as both were issued very sparingly and nibs were only replaced when they were very badly 'crossed'. Inky fingers were very much an occupational hazard at this time. Ink, always Stephens, was kept in large brown earthenware bottles in the teacher's cupboard and eventually I rose to the dizzy heights of being one of two ink monitors whose job it was to fill up all the inkwells in the classroom every morning. It was not until we were in the 'top class' that we were permitted to bring in our own fountain pens. Ballpoint pens didn't appear until the very late 1940s, were initially quite a luxury and would certainly not have been permitted at school. When dad got his first Biro it looked like a fairly posh fountain pen and was kept in its case in his desk and was only used for writing letters or for important forms.

As I have said, pens, paper and other consumables were in

short supply and many items were still rationed, but one 'treat' was provided free each and every day at school and that was milk. The milkman would deliver a number of metal crates each containing twenty-four little one third of a pint bottles, enough for a bottle each – and I suspect a few over for the teacher's tea. Two 'big boys' from the top class were appointed as 'milk monitors' and just before morning playtime would carry the crates in from outside and supervise distribution. Consumption was virtually compulsory which was fine by me if it was winter and the milk was nicely chilled or even frozen, but when the crates had been out in the sun for a couple of hours and the milk was warm or perhaps fast heading towards being 'off', I couldn't stand it and to this day I am totally unable to drink milk on its own. Eventually having reached the pinnacle of power as a milk monitor I was able to ensure that lesser mortals suffered while totally avoiding the evil liquid myself.

Miss Freeman was succeeded by Mrs Benfield with hair screwed tightly into a bun, sharp features and a tongue to match. There was not much politically correct or educationally modern about Mrs Benfield. Any girl unable to re-tie her hair ribbon, any boy unable to do up his shoelaces and any child not conforming or doing anything that didn't meet Mrs Benfield's high standards was dragged out in front of the class and expertly ridiculed. You very soon learned how to learn in her class. As the years went by I discovered that Miss Freeman's name was Laura, the Headmaster was Sidney Chaperlin and Mr Childerley was Ken, but to this day, Mrs Benfield remains Mrs Benfield. A few more like her in today's classrooms would work wonders.

There are only two other teachers I can remember and one of

A school 'mug shot' at around age ten

these was either temporary or a trainee and is only remembered because of the endless amusement that we small boys derived from her name – Miss Willy! The other, Mr Hole, came later during my time at the school and I think replaced either Mr Childerley or Mrs Benfield. 'Danny' Hole was short, slight and very enthusiastic. He was a great one for the open air and in the summer would take every opportunity to move lessons outside. He once decided to take us for a 'nature walk' and then thought it would be a good idea if we all took our shirts off – including the girls! The boys thought it was a great idea but the girls were not so happy. Nor apparently were the parents of some of the girls and even I became aware of some of the rumblings of discontent. Nature walks continued but were always of the fully clothed variety from then on.

Throughout my life, I have got on with most people but very occasionally there have been those who I just couldn't stand. My first such was Valerie Tucker. I'm told that very early in my school life I came home saying for no apparent logical reason, 'I hate that Valerie Tucker.' I have no idea why I formed this instant dislike but there were a couple of later incidents that to my mind confirmed my judgement. Valerie had been given the job of walking Mr Childerley's dog during the lunch break on the village green that adjoined the school and I exchanged a few friendly words with her, possibly wondering which teacher's pet was leading which. Later I was hauled in by Mr Childerley and was amazed to be told that I had been accused of throwing stones at his dog. Despite protesting my very real innocence, I was given a right rollicking and later in front of the whole class I was formally stripped of my RSPCA Animal Defenders badge. The teacher told me that, if I asked nicely, I could have my badge back at the end of term, but in an early display of contempt for poor performance standards by those in authority over me I decided that he could keep the damned badge and I never did ask for its return.

On another occasion I was selected to conduct the school band at a concert. Band is perhaps an exaggeration, as it comprised a few recorders played by those whose parents could afford to buy one, one drum, a few tambourines and large numbers of triangles. There was some debate between me and the drum player as to which was the top job but I was happy that mine was obviously number one and a couple of rehearsals went very well. On the day of the final rehearsal I was struck down with an illness and couldn't go to school. On my return I was told that as I had missed the rehearsal I had been relegated to fifteenth triangle and the conductor was now, you've guessed it, my dear friend Valerie Tucker!

Mr Childerley was involved in another incident that must have been a bit traumatic at the time because it is fixed so well in my memory. One day at the end of school he gave me a string bag containing two or three grocery items to take home to my mother to be used as raffle prizes at a Parent Teacher Association meeting that evening. I set off home quite happily, swinging the string bag around my head from time to time until I reached the Duck Pond – no ducks but usually newts, tadpoles and various creepy crawlies which of course demanded a few minutes attention before I went on my way. Newts and the like obviously require the use of both hands and the bag was carefully placed on the grass bank at the pond's edge. Having suitably annoyed all the aquatic wildlife I could reach, I wandered on without a further thought for the string bag or its contents.

On arrival home, my happy daydream about catching the biggest crested newt ever was rudely interrupted by Mum's question, 'did Mr Childerley remember to give you those raffle prizes?' Panic and a full speed dash the half-mile back to the pond followed. I was not particularly athletic and no doubt that day I fully justified my grandmother's usual poetic description of my running style – 'head there, arse a-coming'. Needless to say, the goodies had gone. Worse still, apart from recalling one item being a half pound packet of margarine, I had no idea what else had been in the bag, so it wasn't even possible for Mum to quietly replace them. I was marched back to the village to knock on the teacher's door not only to apologise but also to find out what had actually been in the bag, with my escape route firmly blocked by mother standing cross-armed at the garden gate. I think that Mr Childerley's wife felt quite sorry for me and said she would donate something else but mother being mother, every item had to be exactly duplicated, even the bag had to be replaced with one slightly better and my pocket money suffered a serious reduction for a number of weeks afterwards.

Losing things was not a regular occurrence and two 'lost' items were not really lost at all. On the way home one day, I was playing with my cap, which with the peak tucked-in became a reasonable ball, and was attempting the world record for highest throw and catch. Unfortunately my aim was well adrift and it came down several yards into a patch of very dense and very tall stinging nettles – not the place to go wearing short trousers. Afraid to admit my stupidity, I told a pack of lies about the cap being stolen by older boys who I was naturally unable to identify. What was really stupid was that Dad could easily have retrieved the cap with one of his array of tools, Mum would probably have just laughed and almost certainly they could ill afford a replacement. My other 'loss' was a pair of underpants! Having had a slight accident and again being scared or embarrassed to admit to what was not much more than a wet fart, I visited Aunt Alice after school and hid the pants in her cupboard. A few days later when I had more time, I retrieved them and hid them deep in a bramble bush off a public footpath. This time the story was that I had accidentally left them in the boys' toilets, and I did feel quite guilty when Mum made an after-hours visit to the school in what I knew would be a fruitless attempt to recover what had been a virtually new pair of pants.

There were always animals at home during my school days. Usually a dog, hens, ducks and always at least one cat, often many more, I think nine was the maximum number of felines at any one time. All had to be given names and over the years I remember such originals as Blackie, Tabby, Tubby (because it looked just like Tabby but was fatter) and Soona (because it would soona do its business in the house than go outside). One of my favourite cats was black and white, the colours of our local football team, Luton Town, and was therefore immediately christened Luton. One day he went missing – I always thought of him as he but it could just have likely been a she. I wasn't too worried at first as cats regularly disappeared and reappeared. Very often this was to have kittens. We only ever had male dogs and there was never money available to have cats neutered. I realise now that it was as if the cats knew what would happen to their kittens if Dad found them before their eyes opened. I spent hours wandering round the garden and adjoining fields looking for my lost friend without success and eventually gave up. Some considerable time later I saw a cat in the front window of a school friend's house and told my mother, 'Chris Bird has got a cat just like my Luton.' I was well into adulthood before she told me that it was indeed my Luton – the wicked woman had given him away.

Our animals were sometimes a source of embarrassment to me at school. At one time we kept geese that roamed free grazing in the orchard, which unfortunately was also where Mum hung out the washing. Geese eat grass but are willing to try most other things, so I regularly had to go to school with green cuffs on my white shirt where the geese had nibbled at the sleeves. In later years when I had a bike, one particular dog often followed me to school, nipping at my ankles as I rode along. It got so bad that often I would wear Wellington boots even in the driest weather just to protect my legs from the mad canine. The dog was called Whisky, possibly because there was a brand called Black & White and that was its colouring. It would hang around outside the school and usually after a while would lose interest and look for someone else to annoy, but every now and then it would still be there at playtime when the whole school would go out onto the village green. The dog would then studiously ignore my every command and try to make love to the legs of every girl it saw. Inevitably this would come to the attention of a teacher and it would only be a matter of time before I heard, 'George Jackson, if that's your dog you had better take him home NOW.'

I was always a bit of a loner and usually coming top of the class didn't particularly help in the popularity stakes. I was by no means without friends but one incident led to much wider respect and acceptance – a fight with Laurie Kent. Laurie was the school's hard man. He wasn't particularly large but even at about age nine or ten you didn't want to mess with him. I would normally go to great lengths to avoid any sort of trouble but one day, and I can't remember why, it was agreed that an after school fight would settle whatever difference we had had. Fights were always held in the wide 'boys' corridor between the classrooms and the entrance doors, which was small enough to provide a compact combat area with few escape routes and large enough to house a good number of fairly vocal spectators. This was my first and as it transpired also my last fight in this famous arena and I remember having most of the day to worry about it before it took place. I probably only turned up because my fear of ridicule for being 'chicken' was marginally greater than my fear of the fight itself.

At the appointed hour with a good audience assembled, lookouts for teachers were posted and the fight began. The majority of those present, knowing which side their bread was buttered, were supporting Laurie but I was pleasantly surprised by the number shouting for me. Blows were exchanged with some wrestling mixed in and, doing my best to remember not to 'fight like a girl' (biting or scratching was the ultimate sin), I was pleased to find I was just about holding my own. Early in the proceedings Laurie had missed me with a punch and had cut his hand quite badly on the metalwork of the classroom door. Possibly this had hampered him or possibly he had been slowed down and I had been protected by the fact that we were both wearing our navy blue gabardine macs to facilitate a quick exit should a teacher appear. But for whatever reason, after about ten minutes, Laurie decided that we had fought an honourable draw and that I was now welcome to become a member of his gang which involved immediate promotion from Indian to Cowboy and from German to English in all future playground 'battles'. Feeling quite proud of myself I set off through the village to Aunt Alice's where I was to meet Mum later. I called in at George's sweet shop on route and was conscious that Mrs George was looking at me quite strangely as had a number of people on the way. When I got to Aunt Alice's I was met with, 'good God boy, whatever has happened to you?' I was quite literally covered in blood, virtually all of which belonged to Laurie from his cut hand. Getting over the initial shock, Alice quickly cleaned me up and I was looking as good as new by the time Mum arrived. Any hope of keeping my adventure secret quickly disappeared the next day when half the village asked Mother if I was all right after my accident!

Towards the end of my years at the school on the green came what was probably my most embarrassing incident. Mum needed something from Luton, couldn't go herself and decided that I was old enough by now to undertake my first ever solo bus trip. At lunchtime, I was carefully given the money, briefed on exactly what to get, from where and how to get there. If I hurried across the village green after school I should be just in time to catch a number 6 bus into town. That afternoon, I rehearsed every step of the mission in my head and when everyone came out of school, I hurried across to the bus stop and sure enough, along came a number 6. Everything went perfectly – straight to the shop, they had exactly what it was I was sent for (I still can't remember what) at exactly the right price and there was even a return bus waiting at the terminus in Williamson Street when I got there.

By the time I got home I was feeling quite proud of myself and was totally dumbstruck when Mum glared at me and said, 'I thought I asked you to go to Luton.' I said that I had been and she replied, 'you can't have been – look at the time.' It was then that the terrible truth dawned. In my keenness to get on with my first solo mission I had left school at playtime. I was so upset and afraid of what would be said at school in the morning that my mother took pity on me and rang the Headmaster to explain. Needless to say, Mr Chaperlin hadn't even noticed that I had gone.

My first school report dates back to Winter Term 1949 when I was eight. The emphasis on the 'three R's' is shown by the subjects listed: Reading, Writing, Dictation, English Composition, English General, Recitation, Arithmetic Mechanical, Arithmetic Problems, History, Geography and Nature Study. Three other subjects, Art, Handwork or Needlework and Scripture were graded by comment rather than marks. Those subjects marked were out of twenty-five and in this first report I got three maximums and only two less than twenty. This was enough to give me first in class but only the rather faint praise of, 'good but could be better'. I retained top spot throughout primary school with the exception of just one term when an attack of 'I'm too good to need to work' saw me slump to 7th. The school Trustees gave books annually as prizes and I remember receiving The Bunker Book, which was all about a Chinese cat, By Paddle Wheel and Pack Train, an adventure book set in America, and Kidnapped by Robert Louis Stevenson. Each prize was inscribed by hand on the flyleaf and signed by Sidney Chaperlin as Head Master and Rev. Charles H Fletcher as Chairman of Trustees, although by the time I received my last prize in August 1952, The Book of the Countryside, the Chairman was Francis W Buckingham.

My academic achievements were not matched by any great athletic ability. I have a certificate to say that in 1950 I was second in the 75 yards skipping (9–10 years) and the following year I achieved the same position in the House Relay (Boys). My

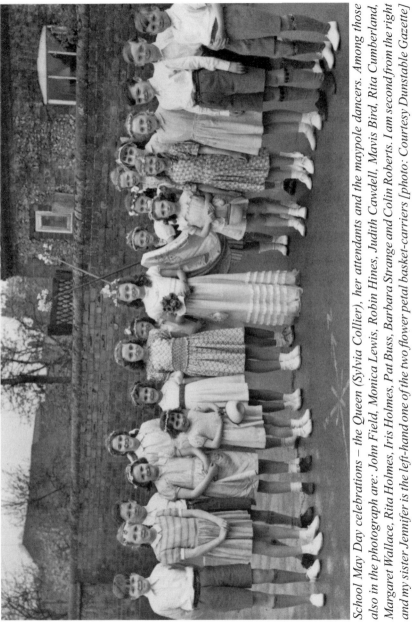

School May Day celebrations – the Queen (Sylvia Collier), her attendants and the maypole dancers. Among those also in the photograph are: John Field, Monica Lewis, Robin Hines, Judith Cawdell, Mavis Bird, Rita Cumberland, Margaret Wallace, Rita Holmes, Iris Holmes, Pat Buss, Barbara Strange and Colin Roberts. I am second from the right and my sister Jennifer is the left-hand one of the two flower petal basket-carriers [photo: Courtesy Dunstable Gazette]

pinnacle was in 1952 when the boys house relay team moved up to first and my certificate was presented and autographed by my hero, Syd Owen, captain of Luton Town FC. Dad in the meantime was winning the Wheelbarrow Race in 1951 and dropping to second place in 1952 but in neither case was Mum his partner – it was someone else's mum whose name escapes me. For the first race Mum was about seven months pregnant with Nigel but I don't know what her feeble excuse was in 1952.

Whatever facilities the school may have lacked, and compared to modern schools we were probably deprived of many, we certainly were not short of open space for games with the whole of the village green available. It was used for cricket and rounders - but under no circumstances on the village team's cricket square which was sacred - except in winter when Houghton Rangers trampled all over it in their football boots! The school used the football pitch and, from unhappy memories of the apparently vast distances involved, we used the whole of that full-sized version. For the annual sports, volunteers used a white liner (and probably caustic lime!) to mark out lanes on the running track and older pupils were used as slave labour to move what seemed to be most of the school's furniture and equipment out onto the Green to accommodate all the necessary administration and what was often quite a substantial crowd.

My talent at football was summed up by a practice match during which I agreed with my classmate Robin Hines that we would make sure we saw plenty of the ball by always passing to each other. This worked very well until one of his passes put me clean through with only a not very good goalkeeper to beat. I latched on to the ball, swivelled neatly and then thumped it twenty

Dad (centre) shows some style in the school sports wheelbarrow race. His partner is thought to be Gertie Bird and the lady to their left with the 'collapsing barrow' is Sylvia Buss. My sister Jennifer is among spectators to the left wearing white hair ribbons. [photo: Courtesy Dunstable Gazette]

yards backwards towards Robin and the defence! But I am still the proud possessor of a medal for 1951-52 League Runners-Up. I was probably the only reserve in the whole league never to set foot on the pitch.

I was however obviously beginning to show a little bit of personality as by December 1951 my report carried the comment, 'a good term's work marred by a falling off of conduct', and in the Spring of the following year, 'although top once again, George's work has deteriorated, mainly due to extensive use of his tongue', and I thought I was a very shy little boy!

3

GRAMMAR DOG

When the 1952 eleven-plus results came out I found that I wouldn't be joining most of my classmates at Northfields Secondary Modern but would be becoming, as they put it, a 'Grammar Dog'. Only two of us at the school on the green passed the exam - me and Penny Brooks; accordingly we were both sent to establishments where we would learn to say Penny Brooks and I. Penny went to Luton High (all girls) and I went to Dunstable Grammar (all boys). There was a co-educational option but that meant travelling miles on a bus to The Cedars at Leighton Buzzard and wearing silly striped blazers. Blazers at Dunstable Grammar were not at all silly of course, being chocolate brown which, should you reach the dizzy heights of Prefect or playing for a school first team at sport or both, became bedecked in ever increasing amounts of ribbon trimming in manly sky blue. At a very early parents meeting Mum and Dad were told that they shouldn't laugh or make fun if we came home talking 'posh'. I never succumbed to that temptation and I never achieved any sky blue ribbon.

The school was located in High Street North, Dunstable, with the main building having an imposing Victorian frontage to the High Street with neatly trimmed lawns and a wide path to a huge front door that of course we were never allowed to use. Within the

27

main building were a number of classrooms, the assembly hall or Speech Hall as it was sometimes known, the Boarders' Prep Room (prep was the name given to homework), the Dining Hall, Offices, Masters' Common Room, War Memorial Library and the dreaded Headmaster's Study that linked through to his house which was an integral part of the main block. On the first floor were more classrooms, the boarders' accommodation, Matron's Room and the Prefects' Study, which was also dreaded, as senior Prefects were permitted to punish minor misdemeanours with liberal application of the gym shoe to the backside. To the rear of the main building was a large tarmac area that we very soon learned to call 'The Quad' rather than playground. Off this were two fives courts and an open air unheated swimming pool. Fives was a game something like out-door squash but played with a leather gloved hand rather than a racquet.

The school was on quite a large campus, the southern boundary of which was formed by Dog Kennel Walk, a well-used footpath so called because it ran across fields to Houghton Regis and emerged near the kennels of the Hertfordshire Hunt, which were off the village green. The path was known to us as 'Dog Sh** Alley' and fully lived up to this name on the occasions that our cross-country runs were routed along it. In this area were the Gymnasium, the Art and Woodwork Rooms and the Science Block. The block was very much the domain of Mr Coales, Head of Science, who some said had been hatched there in an experiment that went wrong. The Chemistry and Physics Labs with their benches, stools, Bunsen burners and smoke cabinets could hardly have changed since they were first built in 1907 and the same could be said of the Lecture Room on the first floor with seating very like church pews but tiered almost to the ceiling. Further along the Dog Kennel Walk boundary was the open air rifle range used by the Combined Cadet Force which, I seem to remember, afforded not a great deal of protection from stray shots for any passing pedestrians.

From there, a long expanse of open grass ran along the boundary with Waterlow's printing works, with its distinctive square chimney and rectangular water tower, until at the other end of the site you came to the ivy-clad Ashton Lodge and its neatly planted flower gardens. From here a path took you past the tennis courts back towards the New Block and the main building. The grass area was used for various activities during 'break' (the new word we had to learn for 'playtime') and lunch. I remember cricket nets, a sand pit for accommodating high jump poles, in which the sand was as solid as a rock, and numerous activities all going on at the same time, even on one occasion a javelin ending up piercing the roof of a car on the Waterlow's site.

Ashton Lodge had originally been the school's own preparatory school with resident master, etc and became the home of all first year pupils. From here we were gradually integrated into the school's ways but we were never able to kid anyone that we were anything other than the lowest form of life because we were forced to stay in short trousers for the whole of that first year. Only one who has ever experienced the pleasure of thighs chapped red raw by cycling in freezing rain will appreciate how good it felt to enter the second year and long trousers and the grown up world of the New Block, which consisted of classrooms and changing rooms that were indeed new – in the 1920s.

Dunstable Grammar School had evolved from Dunstable School, which had been a (very) minor public school founded

Dunstable Grammar School from the air. The tuck shop is front left and behind the main building are the New Block and the swimming pool. Also visible is the CCF rifle range.
[photo: Dunstable School Old Boys Association]

in 1888, and when I first attended there were still a handful of boarders and a Matron who, apart from very occasional glimpses of the Headmaster's wife and daughter, provided the only female presence except the art mistress. The fact that we had a teacher of the opposite sex led to considerable speculation and even excitement - right up to when we saw her for the first time! Another initial hangover from the boarding school days was that the whole school engaged in games on Wednesday afternoons for which pleasure and privilege we had to go in for a full morning of lessons on Saturdays. Caps had to be worn at all times, in school or out, if you were still in uniform and I remember at least one poor innocent being quite severely punished after a teacher had spotted him cap-less but still in a school blazer shopping with his mother on a Saturday afternoon. As a result of this rule, everyone aspired to the standards set by most of the senior boys of having caps that were as shrunken as possible, battered beyond recognition and worn so far back on the head as to totally defy the laws of gravity. These aspirations were continually thwarted by mothers who insisted on brushing and cleaning the caps while you were asleep or even committing the ultimate horror of throwing a prime specimen away and buying a new one.

Uniform was quite extensive and didn't come cheap, which must have caused quite a financial struggle for Mum and Dad. Apart from the beautiful chocolate brown blazers (or the alternative grey suits) and caps, everyone had to have a scarf (chocolate and sky blue), a school tie and after the first year a House tie as well. Shirts had to be white or grey, trousers had to be grey flannel and although not officially part of the uniform, everyone had a navy gabardine raincoat – no anoraks in those days but towards the end of my time there, duffle coats came in and were grudgingly approved by the school. Games kit also had to be provided – rugby shirts white and colours (brown and blue again in hoops), rugby shorts white and navy, rugby socks and boots, gym vest, running shorts and white plimsolls or tennis shoes and of course swimming trunks and towel. Later, if you were good enough to get into a school team, there would be cricket whites, sweaters and boots. In the first year we were easy prey for older boys and Mother had to make a few costly replacements before I got 'streetwise'.

The biggest bandit though was probably W N 'Badger' Brock. In my first year, 'Badger' taught us French with a broad Welsh accent, which is probably why French was one of my only two failures at 'O' Level five years later. In our first lesson with him, he announced, 'you will need a string bag for your games kit.' We all duly went home and told our parents, 'Mr Brock says we've GOT TO HAVE a string bag for our games kit.' Next day, we all placed our orders; each gave him our two shillings and waited expectantly for our bags. He set us some work, hooked a piece of string over the nearest radiator and started furiously knitting (or is it knotting) away. Within a few days we all had our bags and in fairness they were useful and of good quality. We soon learned that he also made shopping bags for grandmothers, bird netting to protect soft fruit and even nets for catching rabbits with ferrets or dogs – all while he was teaching!

Teachers were also obliged to wear uniform, which in their case, was a suit or sports jacket, always a tie and always a gown. Many of the gowns were faded, very tatty round the edges and often coated in chalk dust. The sports jackets frequently had leather elbows, leather round the sleeve cuffs and even along pocket edges to prevent or cover up wear. The only exceptions were games teachers who could get away with a sports shirt and track suit bottoms but even they had to resort to a gown if they were teaching another subject which almost always seemed to be Geography. The only female, our Art teacher 'Dolly' Taylor, wore skirts and 'sensible' tops and, in the earlier years at least, she too wore a gown. On special occasions – Speech Day and I think on the first day of each Term - it was best suits and best gowns and they all wore the academic hoods of their various Universities, which was a colourful sight and actually quite impressive.

The Headmaster was G H 'Basher' Bailey, a former Cambridge Rugby Blue who despite his nickname was a gentleman and a gentle man who only hit you when it was absolutely necessary. His Deputy and hatchet man was W T 'Wilf' Lack, also known as 'Fudger', who went on to become Mayor of Dunstable. Virtually every teacher had a nickname, some of which like J C 'Twig' Wood, F M 'Bandy' Bancroft and A C 'Waddy' Wadworth had obvious derivations. The origins of other names such as F R 'Shifty' Speke and D W 'Bonk' Bishop were less obvious and the likes of 'Muss' (pronounced to rhyme with puss as in pussy cat rather than pus as in wound) Milne, R W 'Slip' Symes and of course, 'Fudger' Lack were unfathomable and lost in the mists of time. Of all those who taught me there are only one or two whose names I could not instantly recall and most I can still picture with total clarity.

'Basher' Bailey. [photo: Dunstable School Old Boys Association]

J D Beresford Milne may not have been the ugliest and most frightening man in the world but when we first met he certainly was to me. His long face was deeply furrowed with wrinkles, a grizzled moustache not quite like Hitler's perched awkwardly above a slightly twisted mouth full of large nicotine stained teeth and his fairly sparse dark hair was dragged back over a head that seemed to have been made for a larger body. A tatty black gown so faded that it looked green, a brown herringbone tweed suit and heavy tortoiseshell rimmed glasses that he regularly took off in order to glare at everyone in turn completed the picture. His quiet, sinister welcome to us new boys delivered in a strange (Irish) accent remains vividly in my memory; 'my name is Milne, M.I.L.N.E. I am your Uncle Patrick who has come here to teach you Mathematics. There are two ways to learn Mathematics – it can be absorbed by hard work or it can be beaten into you. I do not mind which you choose.' Most of us had encountered nothing like this at our previous schools and we were scared witless.

It soon became apparent that there were other things that I had not encountered at my previous school that others had at theirs – decimals for example! Teaching standards and curriculum had obviously varied considerably between primary schools in the county and I soon went from being a big fish in a small pond to being not only a very small fish in a much bigger lake but also a small fish that was obviously struggling, especially in mathematics and science. My parents met with the Headmaster and as a result special tuition sessions were arranged for an hour following Saturday morning school – again probably stretching the household budget, and you can imagine my horror when I discovered that my new tutor was to be none other than my existing nightmare, J D Beresford Milne, the dreaded 'Muss'. He turned out to be not so bad as imagined and almost human, but my new status as a personal pupil certainly gave me no advantages in normal classes where he continued to subject us all equally to bouts of terror which very gradually grew into grudging respect. I fairly soon caught up with the rest of the pack and was able to stop the tutorials, by which time we were in the second year and being taught maths by 'Slip' Symes. We went back to 'Muss' Milne for the two years leading up to 'O' Levels and in the last year he became a different man. Suddenly we were treated like adults and his attitude was, 'if you want to pass I'll get you through - if you're not interested, don't even bother coming to my classes.' In my last term I was 9th out of 24, got my 'O' Level pass and in later life was eternally grateful to dear old J.D.B.M. when I regularly produced pages of accounts, estimates and statistics and administered several hundreds of thousands of £'s annually as Town Clerk and Responsible Financial Officer for more than one Council, without the slightest bother.

Another teacher who earned my never-ending thanks was D W 'Bonk' Bishop who taught us English and History in the Fourth Form. Perhaps I should explain here that, in another hangover from previous glories, we didn't have First Year, Second Year, etc. The entry Forms were Shell A and B (Don't ask, I have no idea why Shell). In the second year we were in the Third Form! Followed by the Fourth, Lower Fifth and Upper Fifth when we took 'O' Levels. The bright ones then went on to Lower Sixth and Upper Sixth for 'A' Levels. Anyway, back to 'Bonk' (no, I don't know why Bonk either). He was younger than average and therefore madly enthusiastic. He always seemed pink and freshly scrubbed, with hair neatly combed but always with a bit at the back that refused to stay down and, as my grandmother would have said, 'stuck up for fine weather'. Whenever he got carried away on a particular subject, little flecks of spit flew everywhere as he spoke and the front row occasionally had to take cover. A regular feature of his lessons was that he would read excerpts from books to us, usually classics, but one day he started on The Naked Island by Russell Braddon, which was all about life as a prisoner of the Japanese in WW2. Initially the fact that 'Bonk' was not censoring swear words in the text and the fact that regular reference was made to a guard called 'Fatarse' caused some amusement, especially as Mr Bishop was rather well endowed in that particular anatomical department, but gradually many of us really got into the book and by popular demand he read all of it over a number of lessons. The Naked Island was one of the very first Pan paperbacks published and then cost two shillings (10p). I bought it and from then on I began to use my pocket money to buy Pan books regularly, many of them war stories such as Colditz by P R Reid, They Have Their Exits by Airey Neave and The Cruel Sea by Nicholas Monserrat. Since then, reading for pleasure has always been part of my life and for that, Mr Bishop, I thank you.

Other teachers remain in the memory for very specific reasons or incidents. F M 'Bandy' Bancroft taught mainly English and History. He was Welsh but not overpoweringly so, bald, large and basically egg shaped. Ironically, his favourite expression if you did or said something stupid was, 'you egg' pronounced, 'yooooooooo eyyyyyyyyyyggggg'. He amazed everyone, including parents, who had not seen it before, not only by actually taking part in the annual staff/pupils cricket match but by the incredible speed and grace he

36

displayed as he glided around the field. His other skills included turning from the blackboard and all in one movement flicking a piece of chalk that nine times out of ten would hit the intended target in the middle of the forehead. Alternatively, if the intended target was in the back row, a wood and felt board rubber would be sent clattering against the back wall so as to descend none too gently on to his head.

'Wilf' Lack, the Deputy Head, once came into one of 'Shifty' Speke's lessons and before leaving remarked to no-one in particular, 'if you want to feel physically sick, look at Jackson's socks.' My socks at the time were fluorescent pink, worn with fourteen-inch peg-bottomed trousers (it was towards the end of the Teddy Boy era). A couple of days later, the fluorescent lime green version was obviously just too much for him and he sent me home mid-afternoon with a threat of permanent suspension unless I wore the regulation grey or black. The aforementioned F R 'Shifty' Speke taught us Chemistry and Physics in a fairly broad accent, which I now know to be Gloucestershire, and one particular incident caused him to live fondly in my memory. In the days when the whole school had games on a Wednesday afternoon, most of the teachers had to supplement the games teachers and chip-in with refereeing, umpiring or general whip cracking at the playing fields, which were some distance from the school with an entrance off West Parade. Even Matron became involved, taking up residence in the pavilion to deal with any minor injuries. 'Shifty' was in charge of a cricket match and I was asked to help him carry a prostrate boy into the pavilion to see Matron. When she asked him what the problem was, 'Shifty' displayed great medical knowledge with the swift diagnosis, 'he caught one in the ballocks.' (That's not a misprint; it's how he pronounced it with ball as in pal and not as in bawl.)

One who never bothered Matron, at least not with minor injuries, was games teacher 'Ken' Davies. He had played first class rugby in Wales and was left with an injury legacy that was a bit disconcerting when you first witnessed the results. He would charge around the field encouraging us to 'tackle low' or to 'step man, step' until, without warning, his knee would give way and he would go down into a heap in the mud. The nearest two boys were then recruited to grab his boot, raise it in the air and 'twist left and pull man' until, with fairly sickening sound effects, his knee joint popped back into place and he resumed his charge around the pitch. 'Ken was quite a hero as, apart from his rugby exploits, he was one of the few teachers who arrived at school in a car and better still it was an MG sports car in British racing green. A C 'Teddy' Towell, who had once played rugby for England, was still playing for Northampton and the Barbarians and as a result regularly taught us games and Geography with a face covered in cuts and bruises had preceded 'Ken'. I remember us teasing him once after he had played for the BaBas in Paris and came back with scratches on his face that we suggested looked more as if they had been inflicted by a female of the species rather than a French back row forward. 'Teddy' moved to Stratton School, a Mixed Comprehensive at Biggleswade, and was doubtless a great hit with that school's female staff and pupils. The other Games teacher during my time was J A 'Jim' Brennan. He spent a lot of his time coaching those with sporting ability and potential – so I didn't see that much of him!

4

WEARING THE BROWN BLAZER

Teachers at Dunstable Grammar School generally kept control with a mixture of fear and respect. One who in my time evoked neither was 'Twig' Wood. 'Twig's subject was Mechanics, which was all about thrust, force and pressure, which he taught with absolutely no thrust, force or pressure. His lessons were generally chaotic and, probably as a result, Mechanics was my other failure at 'O' Level. On one occasion he decided to exert what little authority he had by keeping us 'in detention' after school. He managed this only by virtue of the fact that his was our last lesson of the day, otherwise we just wouldn't have turned up. Detention was rare and not appreciated by us, as many had buses to catch and it was a 'girls' punishment anyway. We much preferred the quick easy options of cane or 'slipper' (tennis or gym shoe) on the backside or ruler (usually metal) on the palm of the hand; 'lines', e.g. write 100 or 200 times 'I must learn not to (insert offence of which accused)' could be done quite quickly if you wrote each of the words in the sentence one at a time in columns. Some tried tying several pens together to duplicate words and those with ample pocket money paid others (me included) to do the lines for them; 'sides', e.g. write two sides on (insert subject) took longer, as some thought or copying from books was required together with at least doubling your normal writing size. Anyway, back to detention with 'Twig'. One of the lads had a dental appointment but 'Twig' refused to let him go to it. The majority of us pretending to rush the door quickly resolved this situation. While 'Twig' was heading off the rush, the rest quickly got the lad, his coat and his satchel through the window and on his way to the dentist. Our spokesman then announced that we would give 'Twig' ten more minutes. This time was carefully counted down by our leaders until at the appointed minute we rose as one and headed for the door with 'Twig', arms outstretched, edging backwards towards the door shouting, 'I will not be ruled by a mob. I will not be ruled by a mob.' At which precise point the door burst open and Deputy Head 'Fudger' Lack appeared with black suit and black gown looking a bit like Count Dracula and asked, 'have you got a problem Mr Wood?' 'No, Mr Lack, these boys have just finished detention' was the swift reply. Strangely, by the time my brother Nigel got to the school ten years after me, Mr Wood had become the equivalent of our 'Muss' Milne and was the most feared disciplinarian in the establishment. Other things were also different as by then they had sunk to the common depths of black blazers!

Two of the few teachers whose names initially escaped me were encountered in my first year. One taught us English and History and was our House Master. We didn't actually join a proper House until our second year and all first-years in Shell A and Shell B were deemed to be in 'Shell' House. He was short, square, signed my report J G M and introduced me to corporal punishment. I am now reminded that his name was Matthewman. His weapon of choice was a wide steel ruler applied to the palm of the hand with sufficient force to raise a welt of considerable dimensions, and his skill was to pause just long enough between the three strokes to ensure that the pain from one had almost reached a crescendo before the initial numbing of the next blow. The pain could last for a long, long time, which is probably why I couldn't remember his name straight away and also probably why I have always had an initial distrust of men below average height. The second I now know to be Fred Cadle and was the first of a number to try to teach me Latin. I could never see the point of learning a dead language and dropped it as soon as that was an option, but in actual fact it wasn't quite dead as we still spoke it in the first year. When the register was read we had to say 'adsum' which was apparently Latin for 'I am present' and when we were engaged in any dodgy activity, those on the look-out for teachers, prefects or other authority figures were 'keeping cavey' and shouted 'cavey' which derived from the Latin 'caveat' meaning 'beware' if any such approached.

L A 'Les' Boskett, who was also known as 'Toss' or 'Tosser' (apparently derived from his younger day skills in throwing chalk) taught Mathematics and also played the piano at assembly. He was rumoured to enjoy a pint or two at lunchtimes and we were convinced that when we sniffed the piano keys when nobody was looking we could actually detect the fumes of Pale Ale.

J V 'Jim' Horwood taught Geography and my main memory of him comes from a school trip to Switzerland, which was the first time that I had ever been across the sea or up anything higher than Snowdon. We were in a coach that was like no coach that we had ever seen because its rear wheels were near the middle so that the back of the coach could hang out in space as we went round hairpin bends. We were navigating a never-ending series of hairpins high in the Swiss Alps when Jim, who was sitting next to the driver, decided to try out his conversational French on him. I shall never forget the increasing look of horror on Jim's face as the driver in a very long response demonstrated that he was totally incapable of speaking without vastly expressive gestures with both hands at once and only occasionally and at the last possible moment returned one hand to the steering wheel to negotiate the next bend. Jim's relief when the driver finally shut up was almost comical.

Going to Switzerland meant that I was the first ever member of my family to possess a passport. Passports then were black with very stiff covers and much more impressive than today's floppy Euro versions. Immigration officials were far more liberal with rubber-stamped visas and we were quite disappointed when we briefly crossed into Italy and failed to collect another new stamp. Mention of this school trip reminds me of how very different things were then. I had bought little presents for the family and packed them all in a small khaki haversack, which I managed to leave on the deck of the ferry. I was understandably upset, not least at the thought of wasting all that money. Mum wrote to British Railways who operated cross-channel ferries in those days and about a week afterwards one of their delivery lorries pulled up at The Hyde with the missing haversack and contents all intact. The leg of a little jewel box I had bought for Gran Maud in Chamonix was slightly bent but that was soon put right.

W D 'Codseye' Coales was Senior Science Master and taught us Chemistry. He seemed absolutely ancient to us and indeed he was, as I have since discovered that he first taught at the school in 1909 and was way past retirement age when he finally left in 1959. His

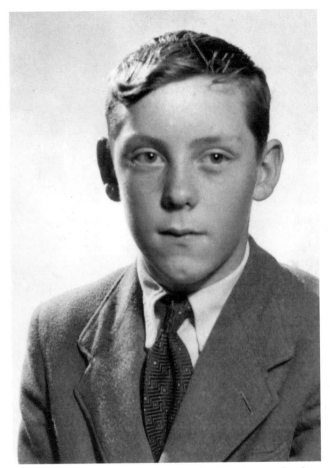

My passport photo for the school trip to Switzerland

Chemistry experiments didn't always go right which caused some amusement but one that did gave us a long lasting catch phrase. Distracted in the middle of an experiment by a misbehaving pupil, he came out with what was for him quite strong language, 'damn you boy you've ruined the whole blasted experiment.' The next lesson we had with him covered the analysis of the experiment and right at the start 'Codseye' made the somewhat unexpected

43

announcement that, 'yesterday's results are the best I've had for over thirty years.' From then on, 'you've ruined the whole blaaaasted experiment' became part of our everyday language.

W D Coales serving the school for fifty years with just a two-year break in the 1920s prompted me to check the service records of others who taught me. It was obviously not a bad school to be at, as F M Bancroft, W N Brock, F Cadle, F R Speke, R H Symes and A C Wadsworth were all at the school for over thirty years. L A Boskett taught for 39 years and was previously a pupil and W T Lack retired after 41 years there.

As I have suggested earlier, Art teacher 'Dolly' Taylor was not a leader in the glamour stakes, but her boobs did create considerable interest and even financial reward. It was rumoured that she wore an inflatable bra, which, believe it or not, were available in those days, and there was a legend that one of the boys had actually caught her in the act of topping-up one side by blowing into a small plastic tube. I cannot say whether any of this had any basis in fact, but her breasts did seem to vary in size and precise location and before going into her class bets were often laid as to whether right or left would be higher today.

'Ray' Warwick was a Music master who taught us for a couple of years, during which time he left me with just two pieces of invaluable knowledge. He told us that should we ever be playing a concert solo and have the misfortune to play a wrong note we must not try to cover it up but rather emphasise it, as the majority of the audience wouldn't have a clue it was a wrong note anyway. On another occasion he had asked for questions and, obviously looking for brownie points, I asked what I thought was quite an intelligent question – 'why do French Horn players always put their hand inside the mouth of the instrument?' - only to receive the unexpected put down, 'how else are they going to hold the damned things?'

As I have said, 'Badger' Brock was very Welsh and made rabbit nets, so when on a family holiday in North Wales I came across a phrase book which included the Welsh for poacher, rabbit, village idiot, nets, drunkard, etc. it just had to be put to good use. I therefore spent the whole of a break preceding one of Badger's lessons covering the blackboard in suitably insulting phrases in pidgin Welsh. The result was unexpectedly spectacular – he went absolutely ballistic as soon as he saw it and was so wound up that I thought it safest not to confess when he demanded to know who had done it. Eventually with no one owning up, he took the unprecedented step of sending for the Headmaster. 'Basher' Bailey duly arrived and as soon as he posed the question I put my hand up. I saw 'Badger' coming towards me with eyes blazing and was more than a little relieved when 'Basher' quickly said, 'I'll deal with this Mr Brock. Jackson; my study; now.' I followed him across to the main building and after the statutory ten-minute wait outside the study I was invited in and asked what it was I had written on the board. As I started to translate one or two gems such as, 'Badger is an old poacher' and 'Badger is a drunken Welshman', 'Basher' seemed to be having a little trouble keeping a straight face. When I finished he told me that insulting Mr Brock was a very serious matter and he would have to punish me. As he spoke, I was thinking of the possible options – cane, cricket bat, slipper, sides or lines. Eventually, he passed sentence, 'pick up litter for ten minutes after school.'

A couple of years later, two of us had decided that watching

Luton Town in a 5th Round F A Cup replay was a much better option than an afternoon in school and got on a bus to Kenilworth Road. It was a good game, Luton won and we had some fairly watertight reasons lined up for our afternoon absence. It came as a shock therefore when at morning assembly, before we had had a chance to test our excuses; our names were read out for 'Headmaster's study before classes'. As we were asked to stand in front of his desk, 'Basher' Bailey smiled and said, 'gentlemen I won't ask you where you were yesterday afternoon - I don't need to.' He then slowly unfolded the copy of the Daily Mail that was on his desk and pointed to a large photograph on the back page captioned, Action from yesterday's replay at Luton and a section of the large crowd. You don't need to ask which two faces featured prominently at the front of the crowd. This time the litter picking went from ten to twenty minutes and I think we both had to write match reports.

Most schools with a fairly long history normally have lengthy lists of illustrious old boys. We had only three and that went down to two while I was there. The first was the actor Sam Kydd who at that time and for years later was in just about every British war film ever made. The most famous was Gary Cooper, star of countless cowboy films including High Noon. Gary was born in the USA but was from local stock. His mother was a member of the Freeman family, who ran both of Houghton Regis' corn mills. Gary (real name Frank James Cooper) was sent back to England to be educated along with his elder brother Arthur Leroy and both were baptised at All Saints Church in December 1911 when Gary was ten and his brother sixteen. My first teacher at primary school, Laura Freeman, was Gary's cousin and also his Godmother. The unluckiest old boy was politician Khawaja Nazimuddin. He became Prime Minister of Pakistan and was invited over to attend an annual Speech Day at the school. His visit was a great success but there was a coup while he was away and we heard that when he got back they had shot him. It wasn't actually that extreme, as I now find that he died of natural causes a few years later but he was certainly out of a job. There must have been something about Speech Day, because one year the then Duke of Bedford was the star turn. He made a rousing speech about how we must work hard so that we didn't 'end up on the dunghill of life as a dustman or something like that'. Needless to say, someone tipped off the press and the local refuse collection operatives were not too keen on being described as the occupants of a heap of muck. A grovelling apology from the Duke was required to avoid a threatened strike and no doubt the bins at Woburn Abbey were well battered for the following few weeks.

Flicking through my old school reports, I see that over a period of five years I amassed the following incredible achievements: Beginners A, House Junior and House Rugby Teams, Beginners B and Under 13 Hockey Teams and Under 13 Cricket Team. In my latter years, obviously preferring warm classrooms to cold playing fields, I was a member of the Photographic Society, the Aeronautical Society and the Society for the Appreciation of Modern Music. My longest standing membership however was of the Combined Cadet Force, which meant that once a week I could attend school in uniform and then enjoy various military pleasures after lessons. The major bonus was that every now and then we had a 'Field Day' when we were allowed to crawl around in mud somewhere in the foothills of Dunstable Downs wearing khaki 'denims' (before we had even heard of jeans!), firing blanks from ancient .303 rifles and throwing army 'thunder-flashes' at each other. Rather ironically our bloodthirsty leader was Captain R F 'Brodie' Broadfoot who taught Divinity and often extolled the virtues of such philosophies as 'turn the other cheek' while dressed in full army uniform.

Mention of House teams reminds me of my disappointment when in the Third Form we were allocated to Houses, which were named after the school's first two Headmasters and Second Masters (as Deputy Heads were then known) – Thring, Thompson, Brown and Apthorpe. I was allocated to Brown House, which had the reputation of always being last in everything and I did little to improve that situation while I was there. The biggest let down though was the House tie. The Brown House tie was a wishy-washy affair that looked like a normal School tie that had faded badly, whereas all the others were much more vibrant combinations of blue, red, navy and yellow that clashed beautifully with the chocolate brown blazers. Another disappointment was that my hockey wasn't good enough to go on representing the school beyond Under 13 level. Had I done so I could have participated in the most eagerly awaited event of the year – the match against the GIRLS of Luton High.

What with being the only one from my village in my year (David Calcott was a year or possibly two ahead but it just wasn't done for a Third or Fourth Former to even acknowledge the existence of a First Year) and being initially a bit out of my depth academically, I was a bit of a loner until around age thirteen when Tony Toombs came to the school and became my best mate; later he became a workmate and subsequently Best Man at my wedding. It's a bit sad I suppose that I could only remember the names of a handful of boys in my class until I refreshed my memory and a bit worrying that, of those I could remember, one left early to go to ballet school and another, until his voice eventually broke, regularly enjoyed taking the female lead in the school play!

The crunch finally came on Tuesday 2 July 1957 – my first G C E 'O' Level Exam in which we had three hours to answer any six questions from nine on my least favourite subject, Mechanics. One question I tried read:

> *In an experiment with a simple wheel and axle, the wheel diameter was 12.5 inches and the axle diameter 5 inches. An effort of 5.7lb raised a load of 10lb. Find the efficiency.*
>
> *With the same machine a load of 50lb was raised with an effort of 23.8lb.*
>
> *What was now the efficiency?*
>
> *How do you account for the difference in the values of the efficiency?*

Mathematical tables and squared paper were provided. Slide rules were prohibited; pocket calculators didn't exist! Could I do it now? Definitely not. Could I do it then? Not quite, I just failed this paper.

I took eight subjects but this didn't just mean eight exams. For example, Elementary Mathematics, as it was somewhat disparagingly called, comprised three papers, Algebra, Geometry and Arithmetic totalling six and a half hours; Geography was in two exams totalling four hours fifteen minutes, and both Physics and Chemistry had both Theory and Practical papers. With the exception of Mechanics and French (which I walked out half way through as I knew I was flogging a dead cheval), all went well and I quite happily answered such questions as:

On his fifteenth birthday a boy invested a gift of £80 at 5% per annum compound interest. On his eighteenth birthday he withdrew his £80 together with the accumulated interest, to help pay for a £120 motor bicycle, his father paying the difference. Find, correct to the nearest shilling, how much his father paid. (Arithmetic)

If a straight line touch a circle, and from the point of contact a chord be drawn, prove that the acute angle which this chord makes with the tangent is equal to the angle in the alternate segment. (Geometry)

The sum of the first two terms of a geometrical progression is equal to six times the third term. Calculate the two possible values of the common ratio. (Algebra)

State Boyles Law and Charles Law. (Chemistry)

Draw a labelled diagram of an optical system which can form a pure spectrum on a screen. Show the ray tracks through the prism from any one incident ray when the incident light looks red but is actually a mixture of ultra-violet, red and infra-red. How could the ultra-violet and the infra-red falling on the screen be detected? (Physics)

> *Explain how physical features, climate and mineral resources Influence the occupations of the people in either Cornwall and Devonshire or the English Lake District. (Geography)*

> *Why did Mr Polly decide to kill himself? Write a concise account of his preparations for suicide; and show how events developed which prevented him from fulfilling his intention.(English Literature – The History of Mr Polly by H G Wells)*

> *Read this passage carefully. Make a summary of the passage, which contains 351 words, in not more than 130 words. Take care to give a continuous connexion of ideas, and use your own words as far as possible. Failure to keep within the limit of 130 words will be penalised (English Language)*

How do these compare with modern G C S Es I wonder?

The exams lasted for a fortnight in what was glorious summer weather. Tony and I had decided early that, having worked hard before they started, it would be counterproductive to try to keep on revising while they were on. So while most of those around us sat on the grass furiously scribbling or reading, we spent virtually every minute between exams playing tennis on the deserted courts. It obviously worked because we both only failed the ones we knew we would. I left school on 19th July and I think the Headmaster, 'Basher' Bailey, got it just about right when he wrote on my final report:

> *'Something of an individualist who has ability and who, when he realises the need for study for a particular career, will probably do quite well'.*

I did and I think I did!

The last-ever school photo

5

LIFE AT THE HYDE

The house where I was born, The Hyde, was a new house, having been built only two years before, but by today's standards it didn't have many mod cons. There was a Triplex range in the dining room which supplied the hot water and could be used for cooking but was only used for this purpose during power cuts. There was a fireplace in the front room but this was very rarely lit and the room itself was only used when we had visitors until it became my bedroom in my later teens. A two bar electric fire provided the heating. There were also fireplaces in two of the three bedrooms but these were never lit unless someone was ill. There was originally no heating in the kitchen until a Crane stove was fitted which burned coke rather than coal and when the wind was in the wrong direction gave off fumes that made your eyes water and that you could still taste on the back of your throat long after you had left the house.

There was no immersion heater originally, so, unless by some miracle the Triplex had stayed alight during the night, you needed a kettle of hot water for your morning wash. In winter, the kettle was also needed at night to fill hot water bottles to give just a little warmth to your bed. These came in two varieties – the ones made from china (which we called stone) that went cold quite quickly and could give you a nasty stubbed toe if you forgot they were there, and the rubber ones which were liable to leak or even burst. Both could burn if you weren't careful and I remember Mum making flannelette covers for the rubber ones to prevent this. When it was really cold there were extra blankets with overcoats on top, but we still tended to have nearly as many clothes on in bed as during the day. I have gone to bed in vest, pants, pyjamas, pullover, socks, gloves and even a woolly hat. In the morning we would regularly wake up to find ice in pretty fern patterns on the inside of the windows and remark that 'Jack Frost has been'.

Although the house was fully plumbed with a bath and inside toilet (which many didn't have in those days), there was no mains water. There was an artesian well sunk when the house was built and water had to be pumped by hand up to the main supply tank in the roof space. Dad usually did the pumping every evening after work but if Mum had done a lot of washing she would often have to top up the tank during the day. The pump was attached to the outside wall of the house near the back kitchen window and Dad would have to be out there every night in all weathers pumping away until the tank was filled to the overflow pipe. This was located on the other outside wall of the kitchen and with brilliant architectural design was immediately above the back door. I have very early memories of Mum, having heard the overflow start to drip on to the little porch over the back door, banging on the window and shouting, 'it's over' to get the Old Man to stop pumping.

By the time I started to do my share of the pumping, things had gone high tech. Dad had rigged a ball cock in the tank which was attached to a long piece of string. This ran over a series of pulleys in the roof space before emerging with a plumb weight attached

54

into the small bedroom alongside a vertical water pipe. The pipe was marked with graduations in inches above the mark where the weight would be when the tank was full. Before starting to pump, you went upstairs, pulled the string up and down to get the ball cock moving and when it settled you could read from the position of the weight against the scale how many inches of water had to be pumped. An inch equalled about two hundred pumps and the normal evening fill was around five inches. We even had an automatic counter acquired from AC-Delco so that we didn't have to keep count in our head of the number of times the pump handle had gone up and down. Then came the great luxury of having a wooden shed built around the pump so that, if not warm, you could at least be dry while pumping away. When many years later mains water finally arrived, Mother never stopped complaining that 'it doesn't taste right' and 'you can't make a decent cup of tea'.

As well as lacking mains water, the house was not connected to the sewerage system. Everything went to a large brick lined septic tank just inside the front gate that had to be pumped out by the council as required, and it always provided us with some light entertainment to watch when the 'sh** cart' arrived provided we had checked the wind direction first! I think that the council emptied twice a year free of charge covered by the 'Rates' (the forerunner of Council Tax) but that any more frequent visits had to be paid for. Never one to waste a penny and probably not having too many to spare anyway, Dad decided that 'most of it was washing water anyway' and spent many a happy Sunday afternoon with a bucket tied to a rope transferring large quantities of the contents of the tank to the small ditch that ran from our property directly into the ditch that ran along Sundon Road. To Mum's embarrassment

Dad in the 'luxury' of the pump shed at The Hyde

he would happily break off to chat at length to anyone who passed by, making no attempt to disguise what he was up to. At least the irises grew well at the side of the ditch.

Well before they moved into the house, Mum and Dad had done a lot of work towards laying out a garden and orchard, with mother's mother Gran Maud providing the expertise and, from the evidence of some photographs I've seen, a fair amount of the muscle as well. By the time I have memories of it therefore everything was fairly well established. The area between the house and the road was all laid to lawn and flower borders, with a long line of lilac trees, which flowered in whites, pinks and purples to one side. There was a smaller flower garden and lawn to one side and the rear of the house and behind this was the orchard. We had several sorts of plums – Victorias, Damsons, Greengages and some large blue ones the name of which escapes me. The apples included Bramleys, Newton Wonder, Laxton's Superb, Cox's Orange Pippin and Ellis's Orange. The last two tasted wonderful straight from the tree – far better than any Golden Delicious or other supermarket rubbish today and of the plums, one of the two types of greengages was my favourite. We also had blackcurrants, redcurrants, various gooseberries, raspberries and loganberries.

Beyond the orchard was the vegetable plot where Dad grew early and main crop potatoes, cabbage of various varieties to ideally cover the whole year (cabbage white butterfly caterpillars permitting), including Brussels sprouts and Savoys, peas, broad and runner beans, carrots, beetroot and a huge bed of rhubarb. There were occasional ventures into more exotic things such as marrows and ridge cucumbers and even one year, tobacco! But strangely we never had a greenhouse and so there were no tomatoes or anything else requiring more than a cold frame to survive. You couldn't just pop to the shop for a packet of seeds as they were in very short supply, so part of every crop had to be kept to 'go to seed' and be saved for the next year. When seeds did become more readily available, I remember Dad spending hours poring over a catalogue – I think it was Webbs, choosing seeds for the next spring.

Despite having no cover for the pump for many years, we seemed to have a vast array of sheds and barns. Opposite the back door (which was on the side of the house) was 'The Shed' made of smooth sheet asbestos that was the replacement for a much larger wooden shed which burned down before my time when one of the airmen billeted with Mum and Dad decided he would 'help' by turning up the paraffin stove that was cooking mash for the chickens. This was used for cycles, lawnmowers, chicken feed and all sorts of assorted rubbish. Between 'The Shed' and the house was 'The Garage', a homemade structure of scrap wood, which briefly held a car but mainly held Dad's small tools and personal rubbish and later became the home for my motorcycles. Before the war Dad had had numerous cars and I remember photos of Morgan and BSA three-wheelers, an Austin Ruby Seven and a Morris Eight Sports convertible. After the war he bought a huge Lanchester to go on holiday to Bournemouth but that only got as far as Winchester on the way back. We made the rest of the journey by train, Dad having sold the car to the garage where it had been towed for about the price of the rail tickets. The car I remember in the garage Dad bought around 1955 or 1956. It was a Ford but unlike any Ford I have ever seen before or since. It was a Sports model, maroon, a convertible and had a radiator grille like a Prefect but there the similarity ended. It had huge curvy

Gran Maud tackles the hedgerows at Hyde Park

front wings, long running boards and a long shapely rear end. Dad suddenly decided he was never driving again – probably had a near miss or something like that (Mum always described his driving as 'mad') and the car just sat in the garage. I got into it regularly, pushed it out of the garage now and again and cleaned it and tried to persuade Dad to keep it until I was old enough to drive, but without success. I wish I had it now - it would probably be worth a fortune.

Within the orchard were 'The Hen Shed' and 'The Duck Barn', the purposes of which are self-explanatory and finally, in the vegetable garden section, was 'The Barn' which contained garden tools, stored vegetables and fruit and in one magnificent year, string after string of tobacco leaves hung up to dry and subsequently to rot before they could ever be sent to be 'cured' let alone be smoked! Mention earlier of the chickens' mash brings back one of my earliest smell memories. Bran, which is the husks of barley, wheat, etc. removed when flour is milled, was bought by the sack and a couple of handfuls were mixed up with potato peelings and other kitchen scraps and then boiled in a little water before feeding to the poultry. Obviously on the basis that lightning doesn't strike twice, we still boiled it in 'The Shed' over a paraffin burning stove and the smell you either loved or hated but either way it was unmistakeable.

We always had at least a dozen laying chickens and at one time or another had geese and ducks as well. We also had rabbits for a while and although I watched Dad kill a couple and even had a go myself learning the true meaning of a 'rabbit punch' (hold it up by its back legs and chop it across the back of its neck with the side of your hand), eventually we all got too attached to them to want to eat them and ended up keeping them as pets. On one family holiday I bought a bantam cock and six hens and transported them back home in cardboard boxes on the motor coach. The driver let me sit at the front where there was more room for my boxes and very few of the passengers realised what I had in them until one of the hens laid an egg, started clucking and set the cock off crowing – quite embarrassing for a twelve year old. Both the ducks and the bantams met unusual ends. The ducks went missing one morning and we eventually found a couple of survivors in the field next door. After a search we found the rest all dead but unmarked. We eventually worked out that they had escaped through wire and the hedge into the field, had been unable to find their way back into their shed and, the night being very cold, they had huddled up to sleeping cattle for warmth and been crushed when the cows moved. The demise of my bantams was even more grisly. I went to let them out of their shed one morning and found all six hens had been attacked by rats and were dead. Standing in one corner, battered and bloodied, was the cockerel and in another corner was a very large rat that he had killed in the unsuccessful defence of his harem. It was unfair to keep him without his hens and such bravery deserved reward, so he was given to Ben Tompkins the village painter and decorator who also kept bantams and he went on to enjoy a long, happy and randy life – that's the cock not Ben – well perhaps they both did but I only know about the cockerel.

Good use was made of all our produce. Domestic freezers did not exist, so Mother would spend hours bottling various fruit in Kilner jars, which were large jars with glass lids and rubber seals fitted inside a brass screw top that you filled with cooked fruit in their own syrup. A mysterious process of heating and cooling the jars at the right time caused the tops to vacuum seal and the contents would keep indefinitely as if they were tinned. Other fruits were made into jams and jellies, and sliced runner beans were kept in large glass sweet jars with layers of beans and layers of salt alternating. The smell of fruit bubbling away in a large preserving pan on its way to jam is another sensory memory and I also remember sugar and various potions being added until one of the little test droplets dripped from the wooden spoon (it had to be wooden) on to greaseproof paper at last demonstrated that it would 'set' and the transfer to jars could begin.

Another means of storage was used for surplus eggs. These were kept in a lidded bucket filled with water and isinglass, which is glutinous substance, prepared from the swim bladders of various fish and is used in the manufacture of jellies. My grandmother used it to clarify her homemade wine and many years later I used it in my pub in the form of 'finings' to clear cloudy beer. I assume that it worked by stopping air getting through the shell of the egg and sending it rotten. The egg bucket was always kept on the floor in the pantry, which was designed to reflect the fact that nobody had a fridge. It was a large walk-in cupboard with a quarry tile floor for coolness. At about waist height there was a smooth concrete shelf almost five feet deep covering the whole width of the cupboard. There was a window to the outside with steel gauze instead of glass in the top section and the whole shelved area was enclosed by a steel gauze covered wooden frame and door to keep out the flies. My grandmother's 'meat safe' was far less grand, being a wooden box with a shelf and a gauze-covered door and was kept outside.

For some time after the end of the War, food, clothing and sweets were still rationed and, although with our home produce we probably did better than some families, most of the meals I remember with fondness were, when you think back, obviously designed to make a little go a long way. Mutton stew (never lamb) always came with loads of vegetables and pearl barley to bulk it out and bread crusts to dip into the little golden circles on the surface that were the fat from the meat. Beef stew always came with the same vegetables and 'floaters' – small suet dumplings. Homemade rissoles and fish cakes were delicious, with fresh cut parsley and other savouries adding to the flavour but were probably largely potato. Spam fritters and potato fritters were again very tasty but dipping in batter and frying obviously bulked out the meal. Steak and kidney pudding in its large china basin and liver and bacon dumpling – both wrapped in a cloth before boiling and both using large quantities of suet pastry - were great and also filling. Rabbit, chicken and a roast joint were treats to be savoured. When things became more plentiful, a beef joint for Sunday would be at least part cooked on Saturday evening and supper would consist of bread dipped in the dripping juices.

'Dinner' was always at lunchtime. Dad always cycled home two miles each way from AC-Delco and, apart from brief spells of 'school dinners' presumably when Mum was pregnant, I always came home as well, cycling even further than Dad when I was at grammar school. There was always a sweet, often something with custard, but my favourites were spotted dick, suet pudding (just a roll of plain suet pastry cooked in a cloth, cut in slices and with golden syrup dribbled on), bread and butter pudding with loads of currants and sultanas, rice pudding baked in the oven with a nicely burnt skin, junket, chocolate blancmange with sultanas in, Bakewell tart and treacle tart (breadcrumbs soaked in golden syrup and baked in a pastry case with 'spokes' made from thin strips of pastry twisted into spirals on the top).

The school on the green didn't have a kitchen, so during the fairly brief periods of being sent to school dinners we had to join the rest of those partaking of this delicacy in walking to 'Top School' and back to eat. We had to walk in pairs in what we called a crocodile (none of this 'walking bus' nonsense). As far as I can remember the food wasn't bad, apart from the cabbage, which seemed to be boiled for hours and could often be smelt wafting in the breeze when we were only half way up the High Street. Nothing came up to Mum's standard with one exception. That was Mrs Boar's special sweet, which was a chocolate flavoured fudge type concoction mixed with cornflakes, pressed into a shallow tray and cut up into enormous squares after it had set. Sister Jennifer and I both raved about it and Mum tried to replicate it for us when we were dining back at home, but her version never quite matched up to Mrs Boar's amazing crunchy.

In the early days breakfast and tea were also major events. Breakfast was always taken at the kitchen table, which had wooden legs but a white enamelled metal top that was always covered with a cloth of some sort. In winter there was usually porridge, often slow cooked the night before in a double saucepan so that it was really smooth and delicious with milk and sprinkled sugar. Boiled eggs with bread and butter 'soldiers' for dipping often followed. Sometimes they were duck eggs, which had a blue tinge to the whites. Baked beans on toast became a favourite for a while after a Canadian transport convoy was held up in Sundon Road and Mum was given a huge tin of beans in exchange for the brew of tea she had provided for the occupants of a couple of trucks. From then on baked beans were always referred to as 'soldiers beans'. When we had bacon it had real taste and smell and could be cooked in its own fat, not like the water-filled rashers of today. The bacon fat would be kept in a cup separate from the lard and dripping basins and was very tasty when heated and poured over young broad beans. It was one breakfast time that I saw Mum move faster that I had ever seen before. It was not long after Jennifer had started school. I was already at the breakfast table but there was no sign of Jennifer and Mum had called her several times. Eventually she went into the hall and called up, 'come on Jennifer, you'll be late for school.' Back came the instant response, 'who f***ing cares', and it was then that mother broke the world record for stair climbing!

Tea was always in the living room at the dining table that by the time we came home from school was always covered in a sparkling white cloth and neatly set for tea with cutlery, plates and cups and saucers. Sandwiches were usually of jam but could sometimes be cheese, fish paste or ham with tomatoes or cucumber sliced in vinegar. There would be biscuits or more usually home made sponge cake again with jam or 'rock' cakes with currants and sultanas and the occasional tasty little bit of peel or 'butterfly' cakes with butter icing or jam tarts. As you can tell we were never short of homemade jam. It was always a very civilized meal. Sometimes one of Mum's friends such as Kate Bright or Joyce Chant would be there and then the best china would come out. We very soon learned not to say 'what are you using these cups for, Mum?'

Coming home for dinner from grammar school was well worth the five mile round trip but did have an embarrassing result one day. I usually cycled back to school together with Dad until we got to the A5 when he turned right for AC-Delco and I turned left for school. One day we were riding two abreast with me on the inside and were deep in conversation – probably arguing about football. We had turned the Top School corner past Townsend Farm and we were somewhere opposite Townsend Terrace when there was a thump and I found myself flying through the air. I had ridden straight into the back of a parked Morris Minor convertible and I ended up spread-eagled across the hood. At that very moment, the owner came out from his house in the terrace and as he approached his car the hood, almost in slow motion, collapsed under my weight and I sank down until I was resting on the top of the front seats. The Old Man, in typical fashion, had carried on head down into the wind and was yards up the road before he noticed that I wasn't there any more. I eventually scrambled off and remounted my bike which now had virtually straight front forks and a slightly egg shaped wheel, leaving the poor car owner staring forlornly at his redesigned car.

6

COUNTRY PURSUITS

Nothing much seemed to change at home in my first dozen or so years, so many of the memories I have recorded are probably not in strict chronological order. There were changes, of course, the three main ones probably being the arrival of sister Jennifer in January 1945, sister Margaret in November 1949 and finally brother Nigel in September 1951, but it's probably a tribute to our parents that life seemed to carry on without major disruption in a seamless sort of way. Another change was that there was some limited contact with Dad's family. I recall his sister, Aunt Ede, coming to stay a couple of times. I remember her strong Birmingham accent (Dad had virtually lost his) and her being a bit of a worrier. The children of Hetty, another of Dad's sisters, and my only cousins also came to the Hyde. Twins Betty and Beryl came to stay and Ken, my hero because he had a motorbike, also called in a few times.

Jennifer's arrival brought some advantages, the first being visits to the Clinic, which I think was somewhere near the Methodist Chapel in the village. While she was in the queue to be weighed and checked over I was allowed a sticky bun and a glass of orange, which tasted different to anything else available at the time. We called it, with great originality, 'Clinic Orange'. It

With Jennifer on Ken Pane's Royal Enfield

came in concentrated form in a square shaped bottle something like a medicine bottle and I think it was National, the Ministry of Food brand that replaced commercial brands for a number of products during and for some time after the War. There was also National Dried Milk and National Margarine, which Mum likened to 'axle grease', and I remember it being quite an event when this disappeared and we had the vast choice of two – Kraft or Stork.

Jennifer was considered to be a bit 'poorly' and wasn't putting on enough weight, so she continued to get the Clinic Orange even when she was a toddler and I could always nag Mum into giving me at least a small share. Jennifer also got Virol, which was a brown sticky goo like sweet Marmite, came in a tall brown glass jar like an elongated Marmite jar and was taken by the spoonful, Minidex, also taken by the spoonful but liquid, and Milo, which was a drink made with milk a bit like Horlicks. With all these I usually managed to talk my way into at least a taste. The other bonus was that Jennifer had to go to Dunstable for sessions under a 'sun ray lamp' and I was allowed to join in, stripping to underpants, donning little black goggles and sitting on a rug with Jennifer and a couple of other kids, basking in the rays of what I suppose was a

New arrival Jennifer in my old pram. Dad got into trouble with Mum for taking the photo with me still wearing Wellington boots

forerunner of a sun bed.

Jennifer will tell you that I used to take advantage of her by persuading her to swap her small money (sixpence or threepenny bit) for my big money (penny or halfpenny) but she was soon far too streetwise for that – or, as Gran Maud said, 'as cunning as a cart load of monkeys'. In any event, if I did trick her occasionally she more than got her own back over the years. In the middle of an argument she would slap her own arm, burst into amazingly realistic tears, and shout 'Mum, he's hit me again' whereupon Mum would often appear, give me a quick clip round the ear and disappear back to her cooking or housework, leaving me with a sore head and Jennifer with a broad grin. But most of the time we got on OK.

A couple more stories about Jennifer spring to mind before I move on. As a toddler she had a little doll's pram that was a favourite toy, especially in the garden. Gran Maud was visiting and as usual was much happier outside doing something rather than sitting in the house. Jennifer was charging around with her doll's pram and trundling up behind Maud she caught her right behind the knees with the pram. As you will know if you have ever been hit behind the knees, there is only one way that you are going and that is down, which Maud did in a fairly spectacular heap. After Mum had come to help Maud back up she started to give Jennifer a telling-off, only to be met with 'it wasn't me; it was my babbies going too fast in their pram.' On another occasion our visitor was 'Phippy', Dad's friend and work supervisor Harold Phipps. He had a soft spot for Jennifer and used to call her 'my little gal' in his broad Brummigan accent. Jennifer was in bed but was sewing rather than sleeping and Phippy decided to go up and

Jennifer in angelic mode and me in my best suit around 1948.
[photo: Dixon Studios Ltd]

say goodnight to her before he left. He was always the comedian and decided to tease her by pretending to intend to get in bed with her. He took his jacket off and then his tie, at which point Jennifer told him that she would stick her needle in him if he tried to get in. 'You wouldn't do that to me,' said Phippy as he approached the bed. He should have listened, because as soon as he was in range she did. Everybody laughed, even Phippy after he got over the shock and the pain.

At home there was no TV, no record player until I got my Dansette when I was about thirteen and computers had not even been heard of, so what did we do? The main thing was that unless we were at school or eating a meal or unless it was dark or pouring with rain, we were normally OUT. Hanging around the house on fine days was not encouraged. We had a large garden, we were surrounded by countryside, we had legs and later bikes – there was always something to do.

On walks across fields and along footpaths with Gran Maud we would learn about the different flowers, plants and trees, to recognise birds by their plumage and by their song, with memory joggers such as a little bit of bread and no cheese representing the song of the yellowhammer, and to look for signs of animals having passed through or having made kills. More often than not it was just the two of us or me on my own – there were no worries about kids going unaccompanied anywhere in those days and we could walk the fields, footpaths, lanes and roads or go miles on our bikes without the slightest worry, provided that we were back at about the time we had promised.

Gathering something was normally the purpose or the by-product of our country rambles. In the spring, bluebells, hazel catkins and pussy willows (willow catkins) would be picked for Mum to put in a vase in the house. We would also go 'bird nesting' and (shock horror!) collect eggs, but we would only take one from each nest unless they were jackdaws or magpies, in which case they would either be smashed or, better still, be carefully pricked so that they would 'addle' and the birds would waste time sitting on eggs that would never hatch. This was because jackdaws and magpies were considered to be pests, stealing from the garden and eating the eggs of songbirds. The eggs we collected would be carefully pricked at each end with a pin, which would be pushed well in to burst the yolk and the egg would then be 'blown' – literally blowing into the hole at one end until all the contents came out of the other. Occasionally you would blow too hard or hold too tight, particularly with the smaller ones such as sparrows or tits, and the shell would break, but if the 'blow' was successful the egg would join the collection stored on a bed of cotton wool in a shallow cardboard box – ideally an empty box of fifty Players or Senior Service cigarettes, as these had a hinged lid (only posh people had wooden boxes or cabinets).

Later in the year we would look for mushrooms, hazel nuts, sloes, crab apples and, of course, blackberries. Blackberrying was usually undertaken to eat them until we were stuffed, but often we would be joined by Aunty Rose in the week or Mum and Dad at weekends when we would pick as many as possible for stewing with apples, making into pies or for jam or bottling. Sometimes the gathering was more organised and involved the whole family. One year we got permission to go into the Glebe Field, which was next to The Hyde, to gather various types of wild flowers including yarrow. Several sacks stuffed full of plants were collected, all carefully separated by type – I think cornflowers were included and even the yarrow had to be sorted into white and pink. The sacks were then all roped to Dad's bike and he pushed (no room to get on and ride) the whole lot to Dunstable, where the chemists Flemings & Marchant or Heringtons bought them by weight. We were picking by hand, the yarrow was very tough and, to this day, I still have a lump on the middle finger of my right hand left over from the blister cum callous I acquired that weekend. I don't remember what my share of the cash was, but it can't have been much because we didn't bother doing it again the following year.

Gran Maud made wine out of just about everything and I recall picking elderflowers and elderberries (remembering that if you picked all the flowers there wouldn't be any berries!) and also dandelion flowers for her. She also used anything she could get free or cheap, including parsnips and blackberries. I used to help her from time to time and when I was fourteen I helped her rack off and bottle some orange wine. As we worked, she remarked 'this stuff looks good – we'll put a few bottles down for when you're twenty-one.' Seven years later, we did indeed sample it and it was gorgeous – smooth as a liqueur and with quite a kick.

Arthur and Lovell Fensome, farmers from the hamlet of Thorn, had the first combine harvester in the village and it caused quite a stir when they brought it along Sundon Road to cut the one field that they rented a few fields up from The Hyde. Before then, a reaper and binder machine towed behind a tractor had done all the harvesting. This cut the corn stalks off about six inches above the ground leaving 'stubble', gathered them neatly together and automatically tied them up with brown string into 'sheaves'. A man would follow on picking up each 'sheaf' and standing four or five together to make a 'stook', which would be left to dry. Later the sheaves would be collected by cart, thrown up to the cart – 'pitched' by a man with a pitch fork - and would usually be stacked into a 'rick' which was thatched to keep it dry. Later, the rick would be broken up and fed through a 'threshing' machine that separated the straw and the 'chaff' and fed the grain into sacks.

This process was not particularly efficient and often ears of corn or loose grain would be left among the stubble. Generally farmers were quite happy for you to go in after the reaper and binder had finished to go 'gleaning' – picking up the grain that had been missed, which was very useful for feeding to chickens, etc. The advent of the combine harvester which did all the operations in one go, feeding grain direct into sacks or in bulk into a trailer and leaving a line of straw behind for baling later, meant that far less grain was missed and there was less gleaning available but we still went and got a little. Soon combine harvesters, mostly manufactured by Massey Harris, were commonplace. R O 'Dicky' Andrews of Chalton Cross, who farmed most of the land around The Hyde, grubbed out hedges to greatly increase field sizes and would have several combines in the same field at the same time served by a fleet of the new little grey Ferguson tractors and trailers taking the grain to the drying silos at the farm. The best source of gleaning then was spillage from the trailers if they were overloaded or bumped about too much by the casual drivers, usually schoolboys or students, taken on for the harvest.

Several schoolmates lived in East Hill Road, which until Leafields was built was the nearest housing development to The Hyde. I remember Terry and Penny Brooks, Anne and Michael Gadsden, Pat and Terry Buss, Glenys Brooks and the Cook brothers. It was then only a short road, not fully developed on both sides, which left a lot of 'waste' land. Built across the end of the road turning it into a cul-de-sac was 'The Canteen', which had served some wartime purpose, was now empty and becoming derelict and was supposed to be off limits. Inside there was not much left of interest except some enormous ovens and boilers, but it did provide a useful play venue, especially when it was wet, and had the added attraction that we shouldn't be there.

The waste land was the venue for one of the village's many November 5th bonfires and was the 'underground den' capital of the world. Construction of such a den was fairly simple but labour intensive, so every one was welcome at the building stage. First you dug a large hole, at least deep enough to stand up in, and then you borrowed, found or otherwise acquired lengths of timber, old doors, sheets of corrugated iron or asbestos! to roof over the hole, leaving an access and a chimney. The roof was then covered with the earth and turf you had dug out in the first place, and storage shelves were dug into the walls of the hole. Bricks and stones were brought in to construct the obligatory fireplace under the chimney hole and furnishings would be added, even to the extent of pieces of old carpet. Often, once the den was completed, there would be a falling out between the occupants and those banished would start digging their own den which, by virtue of less available labour and all the best materials having already been used, would be much inferior. Such a situation never lasted long however because inevitably one or more of the parents would get concerned about the danger of everything collapsing on top of us and would come and fill the dens in. After a suitable pause, we would start all over again. One incident caused a bit of amusement for all of the parents – except one. We had formed a working party to scour the village for 'fallen wood' for the bonfire and this of course required saws and choppers to help make the trees 'fall down'. Most of us managed to borrow something appropriate but unfortunately the saw borrowed by one of the Cook boys was the musical one that his father Fred played in concerts and had never before seen wood – only a bow.

Another gathering operation had nothing to do with nature except possibly human nature. We would periodically scour ditches, wasteland and hedgerows for empty bottles that had deposits of 1d or 2d on them. Beer bottles would go back to The Chequers or The Crown according to their brewery of origin, which was often imprinted on the glass. The Chequers was J W Greens of Luton, which was subsequently swallowed up by Flowers and then Whitbreads, and The Crown was Mann, Crossman and Paulin of London, which became part of Watney/Mann in 1958. The pop bottles, mainly Corona and R D White's, went back to Jasper Perry's shop opposite the church. Most of the pint beer bottles had screw tops with rubber washers and they would only be accepted if complete, so any stray tops we found were stored to be married up with any topless bottles that were found later. Other pint bottles and most of the lemonades had wire and china swing tops like those found today on Grolsch, and these were permanently attached but had to be undamaged. Nearly all the half-pint beer bottles and ginger beer stone bottles had the usual crown tops like today that were removable with a bottle opener. Some of the more enterprising (and braver) boys used to 'find' bottles in the crates stacked in Jasper's back yard and collect deposits several times over. Mention of crown tops reminds me of one of Uncle

Joe's favourites that came out frequently down the generations especially at Christmas. Seeing you with a bottle top he would say 'you should save those' and as soon as the question was asked 'what for Uncle Joe?', back would come the reply in his broad Yorkshire accent, 'tin arse'oles for wooden 'orses.'

If you went over the rear hedge of The Hyde and followed the field boundary down or went over the gate opposite East Hill Road and followed the track, you came eventually to a small spinney through which ran a small stream near which Dickie Andrews' men had started dumping the straw bits and chaff cleaned out from his combines and bailing machines. As the heap grew, widened and compacted, it became an absolute paradise for rats and some of us used to go there for the sport of smoking them out and trying to hit them with bricks, stones and lumps of wood. One day I realised that I could do better than this. Dad had got, tucked away in a cupboard, a single shot pistol with a barrel well over a foot long and this seemed ideal for the job; the only problem was – no ammunition. It seems incredible now, but I was able to sneak the gun out, take it to school wrapped in my games kit and, on the way home, stroll into a sports and gun shop in High Street North, Dunstable, in full Grammar School uniform, calmly drop the gun on the counter and ask 'have you got anything to fit this?' The man examined the gun and back came the nonchalant reply 'I can do bullets or cartridges - what are you shooting?' On being told rats, he advised that cartridges would be best and I strolled out with a box of fifty. They were smaller than a .410 and proved to be deadly to rats (and probably children) at up to twenty feet. A great time was had by all (except the rats) until Mum found out and went berserk. The pistol was confiscated and hidden away until years later when Mum handed in what was undoubtedly an illegal weapon during a police amnesty.

It was near the rat spinney that an event happened that took away a great chunk of my way of life. I was with my sister Jennifer and Michael Gadsden and we were playing around a very large stack of straw bales from which some had been taken away leaving some loose straw, some broken bales and scattered complete ones. It was Jennifer that had the matches in her pocket but whose idea it was to light a little fire of loose straw and who actually struck the match I honestly can't remember. Everything was fine for a while, but there was a bit of a breeze and the fire started to get a bit too big. We tried to stamp it out but failed and I had the brilliant idea of trying to starve the fire of oxygen by putting a whole bale on top of it. Wrong move – within minutes there was a real blaze spreading relentlessly towards the main stack fanned on by the breeze. There was absolutely nothing we could do but head for home – Michael to his in East Hill Road and us to ours as fast as we could go, shouting to Mum on breathless arrival 'phone the fire brigade, Dicky Andrews's stack is on fire.'

She said later that she was a bit surprised that neither of us wanted to go back and watch the fire engine in action, but we weren't surprised when we were told that all that action had been too late and the whole lot – well over twenty tons of straw - had gone. The next morning we went to our respective schools. I'm not sure whether I came home for dinner that day but, if I did, everything was still OK, but when I got home at teatime the excrement had really hit the fan. Jennifer had found it impossible to go through the day without telling someone that she knew who set the stack on fire and who had she decided to confide in? – only Pete Church whose father Arthur was the Farm Manager for Dicky Andrews!

The phone lines were red hot for a while and eventually a meeting was set up at our house with Michael Gadsden and his father, Dicky Andrews himself and the local policeman Sergeant Millborrow. He took statements from the three guilty parties and we all had to explain to Mr Andrews what had happened. The three of us were banished to another room, leaving the adults together, when we could hear voices being raised slightly but not what was going on. It transpired that Dicky had told everyone that he had decided not to press charges. The Sergeant was distinctly unhappy and at one stage took Dicky outside to try and persuade him to take us to court, but he was adamant despite the fact that this would mean he couldn't make an insurance claim. I was at Dunstable Grammar, I think still in my first year, and I discovered later that he was an Old Dunstablian and had not wanted to bring shame on the old school or to see me expelled, which would have been a distinct possibility had I gone to court. Sergeant Millborrow left well disgruntled and we were called in by Mr Andrews and told that he wouldn't have us prosecuted but that we were all banned from all of his land for twelve months. To me this was a real punishment, but I was greatly relieved by my first demonstration of the power of the 'old school tie'. Some days later, Mother was in the village and saw Sergeant Millborrow, who told her that she was very fortunate to have 'got at' Mr Andrews. She came back with the wonderful response that he was lucky that his own son wasn't with us at the time, as on his last two visits to The Hyde he had smashed several windows in our barn and then taught us how to make firebombs out of pop bottles! This was all very true – so true that our nickname for him was 'Crashbang' Millborrow.

7

LEISURE AND PLAY

In those childhood days I spent many hours out and about in the countryside but, despite the memory telling you that the sun always shone, there were obviously wet and cold days when time had to be spent indoors. With no television until long after I had started work, radio played a fairly major part in leisure-time activities. In those days there were very few stations to choose from. The BBC had the Home Service which was mostly news and current affairs, the Third Programme which was mostly classical music and highbrow stuff, and the Light Programme which was mostly entertainment and was the one we normally listened to except for the news bulletins on the Home Service. Later I discovered Radio Luxembourg, which was the only source of contemporary Pop Music except for the weekly Jack Jackson's Record Roundup on the Light Programme.

My earliest memories are of Children's Hour which included episodes of Jennings at School, Norman and Henry Bones the boy detectives and of course Toy Town with Larry the Lamb, The Mayor and Mr Grouser, which made me aware that Town Clerks existed but didn't help me much when I later became one. Mum listened to Women's Hour every weekday at 2pm and we all listened on Sunday lunchtimes to Two Way Family Favourites, a record request show presented from London and Germany where many British troops were still stationed, and to the Billy Cotton Band Show with his famous catchphrase 'Wakey Wakey'. On weekday lunchtimes we often listened to Worker's Playtime, which was a hangover from the War with singers and comedians visiting works canteens to perform. Saturday teatime invariably featured Sports Report when I always waited for Luton Town's result and Dad took down not only the results but also the scores, as he ran a 'pontoon sweep' at work that was won by the person having the first team to reach exactly eleven goals. I liked PC 49, which was about the adventures of a young Metropolitan Policeman and Much Binding in the Marsh with Richard Murdoch and Kenneth Horne, but my real favourite was at 6.45pm every evening – Dick Barton: Special Agent, who was a bit like an early James Bond and had endless adventures with his faithful but obviously lower ranking companions Jock and Snowy.

These were all in the 1940s, but the real golden age of radio was to my mind the 1950s. The shows I used to enjoy were Ted Ray in Ray's a Laugh, which was a kind of sitcom with Kitty Bluett who was Australian and Kenneth Connor playing a character called Sid Mincing. The show also provided a cause for some teasing of my sister, as one of the Pearson brothers who sang in the show also played the character of a little girl who had the catchphrase 'my name's Jennifer'. Jennifer herself was catered for by Listen with Mother, which came on just before Women's Hour and always started the story with 'are you sitting comfortably, then I'll begin'. Take it from Here was always good and featured a section called Life with the Glums, featuring Jimmy Edwards with Dick Bentley and June Whitfield as Ron and Eth. Al Read was a northern comedian with his own show and always made me laugh as did Chic Murray who was Scottish and way ahead of his time with such surreal lines as 'I opened the door in my pyjamas - funny place for a door'. One show I occasionally listened to but didn't particularly like was Educating Archie. This featured ventriloquist Peter Brough and his dummy Archie Andrews, represented as a cheeky schoolboy. What a concept – a ventriloquist on radio. Did he bother not moving his lips? The show did however feature a succession of Archie's 'tutors' who all became stars later – Max Bygraves, Harry Secombe, Tony Hancock, Bruce Forsyth and Sid James. The show was incredibly popular and was the first to really go big time on merchandising. You could even get Archie Andrews soap.

The three real classics in my opinion were The Goon Show, which started in 1952, Hancock's Half Hour, which came along a couple of years later, and Beyond our Ken with Kenneth Horne, which ran from the end of the decade into the mid 1960s. For me the first two were literally unmissable and everything else was organised around lounging on the settee laughing like a drain. All three were major events in the history of comedy and all three went right over my parents' heads. Especially the Goon Show, which Mum said she 'didn't get' and which Dad dismissed as 'that bloody rubbish'.

It was around 1953 when Mum bought me my Dansette record player and this opened up a whole new world of entertainment. I have to confess to some strange purchases early on such as Flamingo by Earl Bostic, his Alto Sax and his Orchestra, Night Train by Ted Heath (the big band leader, not the politician), Oh Mein Papa by Eddie Calvert, 'the man with the golden trumpet', and even some rubbish by the Beverly Sisters called Voya con Dios. But in 1955 Bill Haley came along and changed everything with Rock around the Clock and I drove everyone mad by playing it over and over again. In those early years the 'gramophone records' as they were called were 78rpm play, ten inch diameter and made of very easily breakable plastic, although towards the end of 78s and the start of the much smaller 45rpm disks, a few came in unbreakable vinyl. One day I bought three records on the way back from school and came home with them in a paper carrier bag on my handlebars. There was a strong wind, it caught the bag, I came off and I ended up riding home with a bag full of small pieces that I very unhappily consigned to the dustbin. Good old Mum went digging in the bin later on, retrieved the labels and bought me replacements.

By the end of the 1950s 78s were a thing of the past and everything was on 45s. My first two LPs were traditional jazz with Mr Acker Bilk Requests and big band sound with the sound track of The Glen Miller Story. Mention of 'trad' jazz reminds me how big that particular scene was around this time. The foot-tapping drive of this variety of jazz music was really infectious and I was one of many regulars at the Luton Jazz Club near Park Square where we stomped away to some great bands. All the big names of the time appeared at the club and apart from Acker Bilk and his Paramount Jazz Band I particularly remember enjoying Kenny Ball and his Jazzmen, Chris Barber's Jazz Band with Ottilie Patterson, Alex Walsh and his band, Dick Charlesworth and his City Gents, Bob Wallis and his Storyville Jazzmen and, probably my favourite, Terry Lightfoot and his Band. Other regulars, not so much my style, were Johnny Dankworth with Cleo Laine, George Melly and the Humphrey Lyttleton Band. But back to 78s, my

84

personal Top Ten of those that I bought – in the order they were released not in order of preference - would be:

Rock Around the Clock	Bill Haley and his Comets	1955
Blue Moon	Elvis Presley	1956
Singing the Blues	Guy Mitchell	1956
Fabulous	Charlie Gracie	1957
Putting on the Style	Lonnie Donegan	1957
In the Middle of an Island	The King Brothers	1957
Kisses Sweeter than Wine	Jimmie Rodgers	1957
Alone (Why must I be Alone)	The Shepherd Sisters	1957
Lollipop	The Mudlarks	1958
Itching for my Baby	Johnny Duncan and his Blue Grass Boys	1958

The Mudlarks were local celebrities. Their name really was Mudd and their parents ran a fish and chip shop or café in Luton or Dunstable.

Reading was another occupation. Mum taught me to read before I went to school, by which time I was already reading 'easy bits' from the daily newspaper. This was usually the Daily Express with a very occasional defection to the Daily Sketch. On Sundays it was The People and weekly we had Radio Times, John Bull and Tit Bits, which despite its name had only the occasional picture of a girl in a swimsuit. Reading was very much encouraged, as for my sixth birthday Mum and Dad bought me a hardback edition of Robin Hood and his Merry Men and for Christmas 1948 when I was just seven I received my own copy of the Bible. On a more earthly plane, Aunty Rose used to bring us Beano and Dandy every week and later she got me the Eagle. At one time I had a stack of over one hundred Eagles – every one consecutive right from Edition 1. What would they be worth now?

My earliest toy that I can remember was a large wooden rocking horse that arrived one Christmas. It was grey with black dapples, had a flowing off-white mane and tail and a red saddle. What I didn't know was that it had been acquired in very rough condition and Dad had spent hours re-painting and refurbishing it. The saddle was an off-cut of leatherette chair covering held on with brass upholstery pins, and the mane and tail were made of plumber's hemp, which was used to pack joints in piping. For another Christmas Dad made me a wooden fort to house tin soldiers. I also had a three-wheeled bike that again I learned much later had been second-hand and carefully re-painted.

My main indoor playthings were Dinky Toys – die cast scale models of lorries and cars with rubber tyres that you could take off and very often lose but you could buy boxes of spares. Lorries, as we then called trucks, were my favourites, as they were more fun to play with, especially the army versions, but they were more expensive than the cars and needed more careful budgeting of pocket money or more persuasive chat to Aunty Gert. Large quantities of wooden building blocks used at an earlier age were now utilised to create road lay-outs and 'garages' that spread out over yards of carpet until Mum decided that someone else may require use of the floor and everything had to be packed into a large cardboard box, normally none too gently, so that they all became somewhat battered and paint-chipped. In summer I would sometimes take them outside and play on 'the concrete', which is what we imaginatively called the area made of that material outside the back door.

The wheels were second-hand but I was happy

I also had a fairly basic Meccano set from which you could build your own models and toys from strips and sheets of metal. It had numerous strategically placed holes to accommodate the nuts and bolts provided to put the pieces together. I had some wheels and pulleys, etc. but never graduated to the vast array of motors, gears and other bits and pieces that were available. When I had children of my own, I found Lego to be much more fun. Another of my toys was a clockwork train set that very boringly just went round and round a small oval track, the joints of which soon became lose with wear and caused endless derailments. I never did get the Hornby OO electric train set that I really would have liked. Another thing I never got was a pedal car. When Mum took me down the village she often stopped to chat to a lady whose boy had an army jeep pedal car. I was really jealous and I remember being totally hacked off as he pedalled it backwards and forwards while I just stood there waiting for Mum to finish her gossip. I vaguely recall having a chemistry set at one time with glass test tubes and little containers of various substances, which no doubt have now all been banned as toxic, carcinogenic or environmentally unfriendly!

Cigarette cards were almost on their way out by the time I went to school but a lot still collected them. They were small cards that came in cigarette packets, usually with a picture on one side and information on the back. Each was numbered and the idea was to collect every one in the set, which could number up to one hundred but was more usually fifty or twenty-five. A wide variety of subjects were covered but the most popular were film and entertainment stars and sportsmen. By the time I took an interest, the only cigarette brand still doing cards was Turf and these weren't proper cards as they were printed onto the inside sleeve of the packet and had to be cut out. I was pretty pleased therefore when Dad gave me his considerable collection of full sets including many mounted in little albums. The civilised way of collecting was begging from those who had lost interest or swapping duplicates with often tariffs of two or three of one sort for a rare one or if they knew you needed just that one to complete a set. The kamikaze method of collecting was 'flicking'. This involved drawing a line an agreed distance from a suitable wall. The competitors, usually two but sometimes more, would sit cross-legged behind this line holding a stack of cigarettes cards in one hand. They would take one card between the index and third finger of the other hand and, in turn, flick the card towards the wall. The player landing the card nearest the wall took all and the losing player had to flick the next card first. Needless to say I was tempted into the kamikaze version. I did at least have the grace to feel fairly guilty when, in a matter of weeks, being a useless little flicker, I had lost the lot.

A less costly version of the flicking game was with milk bottle tops. In those days, milk bottles didn't have foil tops. The bottle's neck was wider and had a recessed top that was sealed by a pressed-in circular piece of waxed cardboard with a perforated push-out hole in the centre. Inserting something like a metal meat skewer through the central push-out hole, and levering it off would be the normal way to remove the top. Once I started collecting and asked Mum to 'save the bottle tops', she, being Mum, carefully washed and dried them before I totally removed their centres, so that they could be threaded on to a piece of string for carrying to school. I had more success with these circular missiles and often won tops from boys whose mothers hadn't been so scrupulous with their cleaning, giving the whole collection the distinctive smell of sour milk. Other one-to-one games played included marbles, five-stones and, of course, conkers in season.

Mass games for boys always seemed to involve combat of some sort and a stick (unless you were lucky enough to own a cap, pop or spud gun). For 'Cowboys and Indians' lesser mortals were always selected to be Indians and it was compulsory for both sides to hold imaginary reins and gallop from place to place. Sticks became Winchester rifles and sound effects had to be produced for these, for revolvers and even for bows and arrows, which had to be accompanied by finger-in-mouth Indian war cries. For 'war' the lesser mortals were of course the Germans, the horses were deleted and machine guns were added to the sound effects. For a third version that I don't remember having a name, the horses came back, sticks became swords and it was compulsory for raincoats to become capes by not putting your arms in the sleeves and only doing up the top button. If you galloped fast enough the coat could be made to stream out behind quite impressively. Games invariably ended in arguments of the 'you're dead', ' no I'm not', 'we won', and 'no you didn't' variety.

Girls' games seemed to comprise hop scotch in various formats and skipping individually or in pairs with a short rope or using an enormous rope with a swinging team at each end and with the rest of the girls, often with skirts tucked into knicker legs, 'jumping in' one at a time to get as many as possible actually skipping. This always ended in a tangle of arms, legs and rope. Girls also played 'five-stones' and sat around in mysterious groups doing I know not what. Girls were very occasionally allowed to join the boys' games but never the other way round. The only mixed game I remember is ' pat the dog', where everyone joined in a circle and danced round before patting the 'dog' who was in the middle. If this poor unfortunate was a boy and a lot of girls were involved, it very often became 'beat the dog' and could be quite painful.

In winter, when the conditions were right, we would make 'slides'. A light fall of snow was best but a good frost on a suitably long puddle would do for starters. Initially the snow would be trampled and compacted in a straight line. Dozens of feet would then be shuffled in little mini-slips until a nice shiny surface was obtained. Participants would then take a run onto the slide, take up a position not unlike a current day snowboarder and try to make it to the other end without falling head over heels. The slide would be carefully polished and repaired by adding water or snow at the appropriate points, and all those with nails in their shoes or even wearing hob-nailed boots (and there were still a few) were banned from the main slide and had to go off and make their own inferior version elsewhere. The same was true for the little kids or those without the bottle to try the big one, which was always in the boys' playground where there was an ideal slight slope. Some of the braver girls were actually allowed in to our playground to use the slide – probably the only time they were tolerated. The smaller, less hazardous slides could be anywhere else on the school premises and on roads and footpaths throughout the village – lethal for unsuspecting adult pedestrians. We were always in a fight against time because apart from the danger of a thaw, there inevitably came a time when some spoilsport teacher or other adult would come along and put salt or grit on it.

The grown-ups of the village organised regular events that gave them a lot of hard work but also gave them and us kids a lot of pleasure. There was a village fete with proceeds going to the Memorial Hall Fund and I think it was sometimes in the grounds of the Hall and sometimes on the village green. There was a procession of floats and dozens of stalls and sideshows that always included 'kill the rat' and bowling for a pig. I regularly bowled for the pig and always wondered what the hell I would do with it if I won it. One year at the Hall Dad was dressed in a full bear costume and was led around the grounds on a chain. I still don't know why. The school fete was a smaller affair held on the village green and for this I remember rides being available on a miniature motor coach provided by one of the local operators. I think it was Costins but it could have been Seamarks. Also at the school were the May Day celebrations where a May Queen was chosen with her attendants and posy carriers (Jennifer's job one year), and all members of the 'top class' were liable to be selected (as I was) to spend hours learning to dance intricate patterns round the maypole in front of a surprisingly large crowd. There were several different dances with the object of each being to weave a different pattern down the pole with the criss-crossing of the multi-coloured ribbons made when you danced in and out and around, with the girls circulating in one direction and the boys in the other. The pole was about twelve feet high with the ribbons attached to a crown at the top. The whole dance then had to be done in reverse to unravel the ribbons before the next dance could start. There was also an annual gymkhana at the Hall that was quite a big event, with bands and entertainment in the main ring as well as the usual horsey girls on tiny ponies running around doing things with buckets and apples.

While Dad was dressing up as a bear, riding on floats and getting involved in various other activities such as playing a charity

A charity football match on The Green in the 1940s. Dad is in the front row wearing the silver bowler hat. Also in the picture are Fred Cook, Mr Foulkes, Ted Todd, Mr Bandy, Arthur and Archie Wallace and Perce Meachem.

[photo: Courtesy Mr Henry Bandy]

Dad (centre) waves regally from the school float at the village fete. Also in the picture are Ann Gadsden, Diane? Kent, Mr Holmes, Mrs Bird, Mr and Mrs Morgan, Terry Brooks and Colin Cook.

football match on the Green, Mum was into quieter pastimes such as the Women's Institute, being a committee member for many years and also being very much involved in their drama group. In 1955, I went to watch her perform at the Dunstable Drama Festival at the Town Hall. It was quite a grand affair with four one act plays being performed every night from Monday to Friday, with three plays and the announcement of the results on the Saturday evening. I went on the Monday evening when Houghton Regis WI shared the stage with Dunstable Repertory Company, Luton Challney Townswomen's Guild and the St Mary's Players. On other evenings, groups came from as far afield as Biggleswade, Bromham, Bedford, Shefford and Hitchin. I went again on the Saturday when I saw Riseley Village Players, Clapham WI and the Bletchco Players and the prize giving. Unfortunately Mum's group wasn't among the trophies.

I remember Mum having quite a difficult part, being on stage for the whole play, having to knit throughout and being praised by the adjudicator for her performance. Other cast members were Dorothy Knox, Sheila Fountain, Jessie Davies, Barbara Ralph, Frances Goosey and Betty Grayson with the producer being Queenie Bond. The programme cost 1/- and the advertisers included Buckle Menswear, Middle Row, H A Walklate Furniture, 81 High Street, Arthur Chattell Cycles & Wireless Ltd, 40 High Street North, Fairley's Stores, 48 West Street, K Firth the Chemists, Bunty Coaches, The Gazette Stationers, Buttons of Luton and the Whipsiderry Café, 36 High Street North. Trophies included the AC Delco Challenge Oscar and the Bert England Challenge Shield. One of the Timekeepers was my Deputy Headmaster from Dunstable Grammar, Alderman W T Lack.

But our leisure and play was not always at The Hyde or even in Houghton Regis. There were days out and invariably the annual family holiday, which would always include Gran Maud and in the earlier days at least, normally Uncle Joe and Aunty Gert. The first holiday I was taken on was very soon after the end of the war in 1945 when Jennifer was still a baby. It was in Bournemouth and I can clearly remember parts of the beach being fenced off because mines were still planted and that, on the parts of the beach we were allowed to use, huge steel and concrete structures remained just offshore to obstruct landing by any invasion fleet. Another early holiday was at Polegate, near Eastbourne, where we all stayed at a boarding house run by the relatives of someone the family knew in Houghton Regis. Food was obviously still in short supply because we took our own eggs to ensure that at least Jennifer had one each day for breakfast. I remember Gert and Joe having to go up endless flights of stairs to get to their bedroom in the attic, everyone counting eggs to make sure that all that we had taken came back to us and Gert complaining bitterly when her breakfast one morning consisted of just half a kipper!

Other holidays were at Jaywick Sands, near Clacton, at Hemsby, north of Great Yarmouth, where there had been family holidays before the war, at Winchelsea and a number near Seaview on the Isle of Wight. It was here that the owner, 'Grampy' Maddocks, went off for the summer to live in a shed while he let the house to people like us, leaving his cat behind for us to feed, but he did call most days to bring the food and check that his moggy (and his house) were still OK. One day when we went to the beach, Gran Maud decided to stay at home and enjoy a peaceful bath. When we got back there was no sign of her and eventually feeble cries

An early family holiday with Gran Maud and Aunty Gert and Uncle 'Joe' Germaine

were heard from the bathroom. At first it was just the females who went to check and found that she had got into the narrow end of the bath and was firmly stuck in water that was by now freezing cold. They failed to move her, mainly because they were helpless with laughter, and as a last resort summoned the male part of the household to assist. Joe told us to wait a minute, which we did, mystified, until he came back, and we all roared with laughter

97

when we saw that he had picked up the garden spade to help in the task ahead. The spade wasn't actually needed and Maud was eventually hauled out, but nobody had thought to give her a towel and all she had to attempt to cover her modesty were two small flannels as the audience that included all the younger generation watched and joined in the fun. Another memory of the Isle of Wight is watching the great trans-Atlantic liners such as Queen Elizabeth, France, Normandie and the United States sailing in and out of Southampton. For a number of years we holidayed in North Wales at Porth Dinllaen and then Morfa Nefyn. The tradition carried on with holidays at Marloes in Pembrokeshire until both Jennifer and myself were married with children.

Day trips would include at least once a year to Whipsnade Zoo, which was only a bus ride away but was still a great adventure. This was in the days when it was a real zoo and not the animal conservation park it is now. Then you could actually ride on the elephants and camels, feed apples, bread and carrots to the animals, watch polar bears on concrete ice and annoy the monkeys by holding up mirrors for them to see themselves in. Peacocks roamed free as did large numbers of wallabies that would follow you round waiting to share your sandwiches. I was there recently and the only things that hadn't changed were the peacocks. No doubt all very worthy and animal friendly but nowhere near so much fun. Another great adventure was a trip by train to London that always seemed to include Trafalgar Square to feed the pigeons, a trip on a riverboat and a visit to somewhere like Madame Tussaud's or the Natural History Museum. Closer to home were bus trips to Dunstable Downs to roll down the slopes and watch the gliders landing and taking off at the London Gliding Club down below and to Wardown Park in Luton where you could feed the ducks on the lake and go into a little museum that included a glass-sided bee hive inside the building where you could watch the bees come and go and do all the things that they do in a hive including making honey.

Then there were the school trips when I remember going to Billing Aquadrome, which as its name suggests provided various means of getting wet, and to Wicksteed Park at Kettering, which was my favourite. Wicksteed were and still are the leading manufacturer of play equipment in the country and their park included a water chute and a boating lake, but it was a child's paradise in that it had dozens of examples of every sort of play equipment that they made. There were rows and rows of slides where you could slide down one, walk a couple of yards to the steps of the next one and so on, it seemed, ad-infinitum. There were roundabouts, witches' hats and whirly things of every description. There were seesaws, multi-seat rocking horses and dozens of other things that rolled or rocked or both. There were swings, climbing frames, jungle gyms and every type of thing imaginable to fall off. There was equipment that suited the timid, equipment that suited the completely mad and everything was either on grass or good old concrete without a bit of namby-pamby safety surface in sight. Teachers and helpers carried a good supply of Elastoplast and everyone always got home just about in one piece and absolutely worn out.

I have two main memories of Wicksteed Park, the first being going one year in a brand new pair of shoes with what was then the new high tech invention of one-piece crepe rubber soles and heels. They didn't slip down the slides very well and I noticed a lot of friction as I went down slide after slide. What I hadn't noticed until

With the pigeons and Jennifer in Trafalgar Square

*History repeats itself — Maggie and Nigel in the same location
with a later generation of birds*

Mum rather bluntly pointed it out was that the friction had been too much for the new rubber material and as the day progressed it had crumbled away and virtually the whole of the heels of the new shoes had been left on the slides. The second rather happier memory is of the boating lake. There were small rowing boats for us 'big boys' but the younger children had little paddleboats. Jennifer, still small for her age, had climbed aboard with her friend Glenys Brooks, who shall we say was well built. The only problem was that Jennifer was at the stern with the paddles and Glenys was in the bow. Jennifer was winding madly away at the paddle handles and going absolutely nowhere because with the weight differential between the crew the paddle wheels were almost totally out of the water!

8

SUNDON ROAD

In the next few Chapters I intend to take a mental stroll around the village as I knew it, stopping off along the way to describe some of the buildings and other features and some of the characters associated with them. It will be an amalgam of memories of the period of about twelve years up to when everything began to change drastically with the Tithe Farm Estate development. There were some changes during this period obviously with Woodlands Avenue, Manor Park and the original Brookfields Avenue being built and later the Leafields estate, so my memories will not be an accurate snapshot of any particular year but rather an impression of the old village as it was in my childhood and early teenage years. To try to give some structure to the picture I shall divide the village up into sections.

The Hyde to Sundon Railway Bridge

The Hyde was situated in Sundon Road, directly opposite what is now Recreation Road and what was originally a meadow forming part of Catling's Farm, usually containing a few very scraggy cattle. The Hyde stood on a plot that was variously described as being just over half an acre or just under an acre and was probably somewhere between the two. It was bounded on all sides by natural hedges, two of which were ours – the front and the side nearest

103

Chalton Cross. The other two formed the boundary with a large field farmed by R O 'Dicky' Andrews and these were neatly 'cut and laid' every few years during the 'hedging and ditching' season in the autumn. Dad attempted to cut and lay the front hedge every now and again, but it was often more like 'hack and bend'. He was pretty good with the 'ditching' bit though and spent happy hours digging out weed and silt from the ditch between our front hedge and the road so that the water could 'get away' and even longer chatting to any poor unfortunate who happened to pass. The fourth hedge was allowed to grow much higher but got a hacking when it got out of hand. In this hedge there was an unusual tree that we called a spindleberry but it was actually a spindle tree, which was so called because its wood was very dense and hard and was in the past used for making spindles. The presence of such a tree probably meant that the hedgerow was very ancient.

The ownership of hedges on boundaries was determined by the location of the drainage ditches. If the ditch was on the other side of the hedge the hedge was yours and if you had a ditch between you and the hedge it was theirs. Cutting and laying or layering was a real skill. Most hedges had trees at intervals that had been left to grow on to maturity. When the hedge in between had got up twelve feet or more in height most of the newer growth was cut back. Straight sticks were chosen and cut and then were driven into the ground at intervals along the line of the base of the hedge. Selected young trees within the hedge were then partially cut through, bent over to almost horizontal and woven between the driven-in sticks. This continued along with trees all laid in the same direction, layered to build the hedge up to the required height which was usually about four feet and then the whole lot was neatly trimmed to a consistent height and width. All this was achieved with sickles, slashers and bill hooks all kept razor sharp with sharpening stones.

Next to The Hyde, towards Chalton Cross was the Glebe Field, which was owned by the Whitehead Foundation or All Saints Church (either way it was administered by the Vicar). This was always left to pasture for grazing, often horses, sometimes cattle, and was let to various people, the last tenant being Mrs Catling. On one occasion when it came up for let Mum and Dad were almost persuaded into a partnership with one of his workmates to rent the field to breed goats but after several evenings of discussion the idea was abandoned; I never knew why. I remember the field as an excellent source of wild flowers, for some good entertainment when one particular occupier used to spend ages trying to catch a horse that didn't want to be caught and for an abandoned ex-RAF tanker lorry that stood for years in the middle of the field and provided hours of pleasurable play.

Before heading up Sundon Road or Chalton Road as it was also known until the council decided that we had better make our minds up and use only one name, let's stop and look at the road itself. It was surfaced with gravel rolled into hot tar and when freshly done – always in the summer so the tar would stay soft, it was quite a bright yellowy colour and even when it faded and became worn it was still a nice golden brown totally unlike today's boring tarmac and grey chippings. On really hot days, even years after the last re-surfacing, tar bubbles would appear that could be burst with a stick and give endless fun except for Mum when it got transferred to clothes, shoes and carpets! Both sides of the road were swept clear of the grit and dust that built up, grass verges were neatly trimmed and channels were cut through them at intervals so that water could run off into the drainage ditches at both sides.

All this work was done by the Bedfordshire County Council 'roadman' or 'length man', so called because he had his own length of road for which he was personally responsible. In the early days the roadman was Wally Upton, a tall man with a permanent stoop. He lived in the village and when he was working Sundon Road he pushed a large two-wheeled handcart to transport his brushes, shovels and other tools and to take weeds and other rubbish away. Later it was Mr Bright, always known as Brightey. He lived, I think, in Chalton and he carried his tools strapped to a heavy old bicycle that he used to leave inside our gate when he was working nearby. He said it was to keep it safe but was more likely to give him the opportunity to scrounge the cup of tea he normally had from mother before moving on. In the evening, the bike was put to another use, transporting him and a carrier full of cut flowers and other garden produce to the Chequers and the Crown where the flowers were very popular with those with guilty consciences and provided him with useful beer money. I don't think Brightey was connected to any of the several others in the village called Bright, one of whom, before my time but talked about by Mum, had the wonderful nickname 'Oh so'. (Think about it!)

A couple of hundred yards up the road was a fairly sharp right-hand bend known as North Fields corner. Off the left of this bend was a farm track that led down across the north fields to Grove Farm. On the way it crossed two very small streams. The second was larger and ran towards Calcutt Farm at the bottom of Bidwell Hill where I think it either joined or became The Wash Brook, so called because sheep were once dipped in it. Along the length of the stream you could often find very tasty watercress.

Carrying on along Sundon Road, on the right, surrounded by trees, was the field farmed by Lovell Fensome where I first saw a combine harvester operate. Also on the right was the well-made track to 'The Camp' – the remains of a former RAF facility. In the small field alongside the track was a fairly large piece of radar equipment looking a bit like a large, curved grey harmonica that was designed to rotate and which two or three of us could move a little bit before it finally rusted-up completely. The camp itself consisted of a couple of wooden huts, some smaller brick structures and a litter of old military equipment – I seem to remember another truck and some sort of tractor but perhaps I'm imagining that. The huts had yielded some good souvenirs like badges and rank stripes but had been pretty well stripped by older boys long before I got in there. I did get a couple of fairly battered brass uniform buttons though.

Beyond the camp on the right there were three, possibly four, isolated houses surrounded by fields. The last of these was more of a smallholding or nursery. One of the houses was occupied by Mr Gates who often passed The Hyde on the way to or from the village. In the summer he was always smartly dressed and wore a light linen jacket and a straw Panama hat but was never without a tie. He seemed absolutely ancient to us and I now find that he really was – according to my grandmother's records he was 94 when she 'laid him out' for the undertaker in 1961. Beyond this and on the other side of the road there was nothing but fields.

Having re-read the previous paragraph, perhaps I should explain what I mean by 'laying out'. Basically it is the tidying up of a dead body and making it look its best for viewing by family and friends and preparing it for the undertakers to place in the coffin. Gran Maud kept records of all her 'customers' and according to those records her first job was Jane Hickingbottom aged 59 in 1922 for which she earned eleven shillings (55p). The surname would suggest that Jane was either Maud's aunt or a cousin. She only did one that year but by 1925 she was up to seven, including another relative, Jane Humphrey. She carried on averaging about one a month until not long before she died, by which time she was being paid £4 or £5 for each according to whether or not she helped with the funeral tea.

Sometimes the family would send for her but normally it would be one of a number of local undertakers who would collect her and take her to the house. Her white coat and little black bag were always kept ready and she once showed me the contents and explained some of the tricks of her trade. She would start by undressing the body and washing it all over, then cotton wool would be used to block all orifices and also to puff out the cheeks if they were sunken. If the eyes were open, copper pennies would be warmed and placed on the lids until they relaxed closed. If the mouth was open, the jaw would be tied up with crepe bandages until the mouth remained closed and the lips would be set in a nice half smile. The body would then be dressed, possibly in a shroud but more likely in their best clothes, hair would be neatly brushed and combed and then a little make-up applied (sometimes to the men as well). Maud had great respect for the dead and took great pride in sending them off looking as good and sometimes even better than they had when they were alive! Anyway, enough of that, let's get back to the tour.

At the top of the hill, the road turned sharp right and off to the left was an old green lane that we called Bound Way. This ran for almost two miles towards Wingfield and Tebworth. Bound Way narrowed down to a footpath in the middle section but opened out again before it met the Toddington Road at the top of Lord's Hill. About half a mile in, a footpath linked back to Sundon Road near Mr Gates' house and this loop was a favourite blackberry-picking route when we went with Aunty Rose. Further in, before the lane narrowed, you would often find one or two horse-drawn Romany gypsy caravans. One was always occupied by 'Gypsy Smith' and her daughter who was 'a bit simple' as we used to say. I'm not sure whether there was a Mr Gypsy Smith but I was never aware of one. They moved to other pitches but spent quite long periods in Bound Way, and Gypsy Smith was very much part of the village scenery.

She was also a regular visitor to The Hyde, when Mum would always make her a cup of tea and sometimes but not always take up the offer of 'buy for luck Lady' to get some clothes pegs or a sprig of heather from the large wicker basket that she carried. Gypsy Smith made all the pegs herself helped by her daughter. A suitable long, straight piece of wood was cut from a tree, usually hazel, stripped of bark and cut into peg sized lengths. These would be split up the middle for about three quarters of their length and then carefully shaped and smoothed to fit the washing line. Finally a small strip of metal cut from a food tin would be wound round and nailed in place to prevent the peg splitting further than the cut. Gypsy Smith was so well thought of that Mum used to ask her to keep an eye on the place when we went on holiday! Imagine that with today's so called 'travellers'.

Another Smith, a relative of Gypsy Smith but disowned by

her, was less reliable and certainly less clean and was known as 'Omo', presumably because of his desperate need for the washing powder of the same name. In later times, he too called at The Hyde for tea and whatever else he could scrounge. On one occasion, it was decided, whether by him or by Mum I can't remember, that he needed a haircut. Whoever decided the need, they both decided that it should be me that did the deed. I was not impressed but eventually, wielding Mum's oldest scissors at arms length, I executed my first and last ever haircut as Omo sat on a box outside the back door surrounded by ever-increasing masses of grey/black curly hair. Lord knows what he looked like when I had finished but he seemed happy enough and 'young sir' got lots of thanks. Years later, Omo started threatening people, usually in Dunstable, waving his billycan and swearing. Eventually he was sent to prison where he became a regular visitor but was clever enough to ensure that his court appearances were timed so that he spent Christmas and the coldest part of the year inside every year. He was none too pleased when one year the Magistrates decided to give him a chance and put him on probation instead.

Just around the sharp corner on the right and almost at Chalton Cross was the farm manager's house occupied by Arthur Church and his family. Behind the house, down a long drive, was the farm where his boss R O Andrews lived. Between the Churches' house and Chalton Cross there was nothing until they started building the M1 that now passes under the road at this point. Dad used to cycle up with the kids to watch the construction work and later the traffic and I used to stop when I passed on my motorbike to see how things were progressing. I remember my first run along the M1 soon after it opened in 1959, which was quite an experience. There was no speed limit then but my bike wouldn't do much more than 70mph anyway. Compared to today there was virtually no traffic and large numbers of breakdowns as old cars never designed for speed were pushed beyond their limits.

Turn left at Chalton Cross and then right and you were at Sundon Bridge where I often came with Jennifer and others, usually on bicycles and complete with picnic lunch, to watch the trains on the main line. The parapet was lower then and most of us could just see over it – for those that couldn't see over there was a wooden rail fence on the bridge approach to look through or sit on. We would listen for a train, watch from the side it was coming from and then dash to the other side of the road to see the train go through and disappear. I remember some diesels but most of the trains were still pulled by steam engines, so we usually came home as well smoked as kippers and black with soot.

The Hyde to The Chequers

Heading towards the village, there was nothing on the left side but the long curve of the hedge boundary of the field that adjoined The Hyde and this continued until you reached the field gate opposite East Hill Road. On the right, set back from the road and approached by a fairly long cinder and mud track, was Catling's farm. An untidy array of buildings surrounded the living accommodation, which I seem to remember was a bungalow. They kept every sort of animal including pigs – a fact of which we were only too well aware if the wind was in the wrong direction! I only went there a couple of times but Jennifer was a more regular visitor and witnessed the birth of a number of animals but couldn't be persuaded to try the Catling's favourite pudding made with 'bisnin', which was the very thick yellow milk given by cows straight after the birth of a calf and before proper milk appears.

The track to Catling's farm came off the road at a point where the road curved round to the left towards East Hill Road. Also on the corner was a wide field gateway, which later would become the entrance to Leafields estate. Just inside the gateway to the left there was for a number of years a caravan occupied by Mr and Mrs Garlick. They had a daughter Janet who was friendly with Jennifer and often came to The Hyde. Janet was frightened of chickens and whenever Jennifer got fed up playing with Janet she would get me to go and collect a hen from the orchard and wander up with it under my arm to scare her away. Inside the gateway to the right straw stacks were often built and this then became the location for 'straw dens' made out of bales, which could be quite complex and have several rooms. Footpaths led from this area across fields to the village and also to Bidwell.

Between this corner and East Hill Road was a tall, unmanaged hedge that was covered in brambles and old man's beard, the dead and dried out stalks of which could be broken off in short lengths and 'smoked' like a cigarette. I tried it but it certainly didn't do what nicotine would later do for me for the forty-odd years it took for me to discover that perhaps I would be better off without it. On the corner of East Hill Road was a bungalow occupied by a couple whose name was pronounced Marsoo but was probably actually more like Marseux. I think she was blind. As I have described earlier, East Hill Road was then a fairly short cul-de-sac with the 'Old Canteen' built across the end and with ample waste land for play activities. It was also where I saw my first ever TV set in action in June 1953 when I was lucky enough to be among quite a crowd invited to watch the Queen's coronation.

Next on the left was the Duck Pond – not that I remember any ducks on it – they were more likely to be seen at East Hill Farm opposite. The pond was only small, fronted by a grass verge and surrounded by an overgrown, straggly hedge. At the back was a fallen tree that you could crawl out on and get above the water but the further out you went the higher you were above the water and the harder it was to reach. Unlike some, I never fell off, probably because I was too scared to go out very far, but I very often got a 'wet foot' when I ventured too close to the edge of the pond in the search for life to put in a jam jar. There were crested and smooth newts, sticklebacks and minnows, frog spawn that turned into tadpoles in the various stages of their development as frogs, water boatmen and water snails, all of which were accompanied into the jar by a dollop of duck weed to make them feel at home. More often than not, after hours of trapping followed by prodding and examination, they would all be put back, but if you had more than one newt they would frequently be taken to the other side of the road and encouraged to race back to the water for our entertainment.

Next to the pond was an old timbered house called Dene Hollow where Mr and Mrs Stuart Smith lived. When we were younger, we were always a bit wary of it as it was said to be haunted. Later, Gran Maud often house sat for them and confirmed that she had heard footsteps upstairs when she knew she was totally alone in the house. The Stuart Smiths later moved to a former fisherman's cottage on the beach at Porthdinllaen near Morfa Nevin in North Wales. Gran Maud and Mum kept in touch and as a result we later had a number of family holidays in that locality. Mabel Stuart Smith was a prominent Conservative and we were well impressed

Gran Maud at Dene Hollow before I was born

when we discovered that she had been invited to 10 Downing Street for lunch with the then Prime Minister Harold MacMillan.

Next on this side was The Chantry, which was set back down a long drive. This adjoined the Chantry Farm yard, which had its entrance just off the Chequers corner. On the other side of the road, after leaving East Hill Road, there was a plot of wasteland on the corner next to the house where Mr and Mrs Buss and their children lived. I then remember a fairly large area surrounded by chicken wire and usually containing, surprise surprise, chickens! Next came East Hill Farm, which was occupied by Jack and Mrs Blow. I also remember a daughter Jane, who rode a horse. On the other side of the entrance to the farmyard was Blow's Barn, a very

114

AT LUNCH WITH THE PREMIER

Mr Macmillan, the Prime Minister, entertained Conservative women to lunch at No. 10 Downing Street, yesterday afternoon. They are attending the Conservative Women's Conference at Central Hall, Westminster. Here is Mrs M. Stuart Smith, of Caernarvon, outside No. 10.

A Welsh local newspaper reports the visit of Mrs Mabel Stuart Smith to number 10

115

large barn clad in corrugated iron tarred black with huge double doors at the front. This was originally associated with East Hill Farm but was later let to various other occupiers for storage and light industrial purposes.

On the northern boundary of Blow's Barn was East Hill Lane, which was footpath width only at first but then opened out and had houses along it before it joined up with Drury Lane. Beyond this, towards and beyond the Chequers corner and opposite Dene Hollow and The Chantry, there was a wide-open space covered in grass and in some places nettles, which was the site of the huge village pond, filled in during the 1920s. Set back at the rear of this area were some cottages, I think just two, one of which was where Mr and Mrs George Nye lived. He was at one time one of the village's three District Councillors.

9

EAST END AND THE GREEN

Continuing my mental tour of the village I shall move on to
East End and The Green:

The Chequers to Poynter's Hill

Let's start with the Chequers – probably a Victorian building
with three large chimneys, a steeply ridged roof, three large gabled
windows on the first floor and a landlord called Freddie Reeves.
When, on the stroke of nine-o-clock, on every night of the week,
Dad said 'ah well, I think I'll have a half,' this was where he came
- not for a half but for several pints of light mild. In later years, he
changed his allegiance to the Crown and then the Red Lion and
from light mild to bitter, but the ritual was still the same and so
was the time for leaving home even though from around the late
1950s the pubs were allowed to stay open until 11pm rather than
10.30pm (summer months only for the benefit of those gathering
the harvest).

The first time I managed entry to the bar was probably for
an illicit shandy when Dad and Uncle Joe made their annual
Christmas Day lunchtime visit to have a couple and to fill a large
brown holdall with 'take outs' to cover the family's liquid needs
over the two days (yes only two!) of the Christmas holiday. The
first time I went in on my own was not long after I started work at

the Met. Office and had been drinking regularly (and illegally) in Dunstable but not in the village. I had been to Luton and, getting off the bus near the Chequers, I suddenly decided to surprise the Old Man by joining him in his den. He took it in his stride and we exchanged a few words as I had a couple of pints and left. After I had gone, some of Dad's drinking mates enquired 'who was that?' As a few of them were occasionally involved in slightly dodgy dealings, he decided to wind them up and told them that I was a plain-clothes policeman. Little did he know that he was seeing into the future.

One of the regulars at the Chequers was my grandmother's cousin, Alf Dickens, and he gave me some advice I have always remembered and often followed; 'when you are young, drink with the old and you may learn something - when you are old, drink with the young and they will keep you young.' The last time I went into the Chequers was a good many years later, again as part of the Christmas off-sales collection party but this time well legal in terms of age. Nothing much had changed but two things make that visit stick in my memory. At one stage, a nearly full pint of bitter slipped out of my hand and fell on to the quarry-tiled floor. Not only did it bounce but I also got down and caught it as it bounced without spilling a single drop. I could have done with a bit more of that dexterity later on when I swung the holdall (I think it was the same one) full of drinks off the bar counter and managed to clear a whole table top of empty glasses and bottles. They didn't bounce but Freddie Reeves, doubtless aware of how much we had spent, was very understanding.

Heading along Park Road North from The Chequers, you passed on the left the entrance to Chantry Farm yard. Along this stretch buildings included a pair of semis, one of which was called Lynwood, Vane Cottage - a lovely old building with the weather vane that gave it its name - and the Police House, before you came to the field in which Brookfields Avenue was later built (and knocked down and rebuilt in the 1980s) and then to Poynter's Farm. The Police House was home to Sgt. Millborrow, who had got so upset about not getting me charged with arson, and later to PC Trevor Davies. Trevor became quite a friend of the family, called regularly at The Hyde for a tea and a chat when he was on patrol and used to look after our dog when we were on holiday. He was a really nice guy and possibly sub-consciously helped my choice of the same career path later.

After the Chequers on the right hand side of the road, there were a few brick buildings associated with the pub, before you came to a footpath that ran behind the properties in East End and up to the Village Green. Next to this was the field that around 1949-50 was to become Woodlands Avenue. From here the boundary of the Houghton Hall estate ran to the bottom of Poynter's Hill with a locked gate in the middle that was only used by agricultural vehicles except when the annual gymkhana was on and it became the public entrance. The whole of the boundary was woodland, quite deep at the Woodlands Avenue end but narrowing to a strip that you could see through to the parkland beyond when there were no leaves on the trees. Going up Poynter's Hill, there were open fields on both sides and you were down the hill and almost to Skimpot before there was any more housing development. During the very hard winter of 1947, a double-decker bus got stuck on Poynter's Hill in a blizzard and was there for days with snowdrifts up to and over one end of its roof.

119

When the first snow fell it was in feet rather than inches and it took Dad a whole day to dig out a pathway from the back door along the drive where the drifts were deepest to the road. By the time that snow ploughs had cleared Sundon Road and he could attempt to get to work he had had time to clear paths to the chickens, most of the sheds and Mum's washing line. Clearing the washing line was probably a waste of time as I have a very clear memory of Mum bringing in some shirts that were literally frozen stiff and standing them up in the kitchen for our amusement. I seem to recall a washing line being rigged up in the kitchen and there was considerable use of the wooden clotheshorse in front of the fire.

The cold spell lasted for weeks with regular fresh falls of snow. The narrow path that Dad had cleared down the drive had left ample snow on either side for me to dig 'igloos' that were tall enough to stand up in. Jennifer was only two but I remember her joining me in my ice dens and helping to build snowmen. Woollen gloves soon became soaked and hands frozen, so another memory is of the exquisite agony of 'the hot aches' whenever I eventually went inside to thaw out. When the snow at last melted there were floods and for several weeks more there was standing water in fields around The Hyde and even some small pools in our orchard that froze over at night to give me the pleasure of ice smashing in the morning.

The Chequers to The Green

On the left towards The Green there were cottages set back in fairly large gardens, but the first main feature on this side was Ben Meachem's garage. There was a small workshop and a couple of petrol pumps selling National Benzole petrol. Also available was Redex upper cylinder lubricant that you squirted into your petrol tank and cost 1d per shot. It was probably imagination but it did seem to make my motorbike go faster. Later a filling station opened on the other side of the road selling Regent petrol and I used to use Regent 100, which was the high-octane version. My main memory of Ben Meachem, though, is as the private hire car driver who always took us to the railway station when we went on holiday by train – usually to Luton Midland Road but once at least all the way to Bletchley to save changing trains. Ben was short and round; he had a big Humber and later a pale green Ford V8 Pilot and in both cases I remember the boot lids opening to a horizontal position and suitcases being stacked on and then secured by Ben using several leather straps. If it rained the cases would just get wet or perhaps he used a tarpaulin or perhaps it never rained!

The next feature of note was the Crown, which was a very old building with a thatched roof and a landlord called Ted Ledo. The public bar was at the front of the building and had an unusual, long, curved leaded-glass window at the end nearest The Green. The lounge bar was more to the rear and this was where Dad took up residence every evening after removing his custom from the Chequers. Among the characters was Nurse Daisy Cox who had 'her' bar stool permanently reserved and a hook fitted to the bar on which to hang her handbag. She had thick dark framed glasses, a faint moustache, smoke-dyed ginger, and a voice permanently gravelled by the ever-present cigarette. She was both District Nurse and Midwife, bringing hundreds into life in the village including me, and was still going strong when my sister Jennifer started her family. Despite her gruff voice and occasionally gruff manner, she was very caring and a wonderful character.

On the other side of the road there were a number of properties set well back from the road: one I think was a smallholding and another was called The Firs. Somewhere in this area someone had a beautiful green 650cc single Panther motorcycle and sidecar that I used to lust after. Next to The Firs were two semi-detached houses built up on a bank with several steps up to the front door. In one, named with great imagination Hybank, lived Mr and Mrs McWhirter. She was Scottish and according to Mum left the tap running all day in the kitchen to remind her of the streams flowing through her Highland home. It was here that I had my first motorcycle accident. I had come from Sundon Road and slotted in behind a van heading towards The Green. The van slowed and pulled in towards the kerb. Thinking he was stopping I naturally started to overtake, at which point, suddenly and with no signal, the driver turned sharp right towards the driveway of The Firs. I had no chance, my front wheel hit just behind his front wheel and I left a black streak of boot polish all the way across his bonnet as I flew through the air to land near the bottom of Mrs McWhirter's steps. I thought that I got up immediately, but apparently I was 'out' for a few minutes. I got away with a few bruises and a slight ankle sprain and was able to push the bike home. He had to be towed. A few days later Mum saw Mrs McWhirter who didn't even ask how I was but complained how much the accident had upset her!

Opposite the Crown was a house built very close to the road at what seemed a strange angle and with the garden running along the footpath rather than behind the house. Vehicles failing to negotiate the bend around it hit the house at least once. This was the home of Mr and Mrs Walton whose granddaughter Janet would later marry my friend John Hall. Between here and the junction with Drury

Lane there were some houses well set back and it was here that the bus stop for buses to Luton was located.

The Green

Going around The Green in a clockwise direction, we start with two pairs of semi-detached houses. In one of these I remember Mr Aubrey Parker, a balding man with permanently stooped shoulders and a permanent curly stemmed pipe in his mouth. He was very often tinkering with motorcycles, one of which was quite unusual, possibly a Scott Squirrel. To the right of the last house, a footpath ran down to Park Road North. Next came a field of pasture dotted with trees that around 1949-50 was transformed into Woodlands Avenue. Roughly half way along the boundary between this field and The Green was the wooden, green painted cricket pavilion – not much more than a shed really that one year was picked up by a freak wind and dropped over the fence into the field behind. It was retrieved and re-built and was improved or possibly replaced later, and it was here that in the early 1960s my brother Nigel spent many happy hours changing the numbers on the score board as the game progressed.

Once Woodlands Avenue was developed, a footpath into the estate was created and was extended across The Green to the bus stop to Dunstable. The footpath into Woodlands ran past two bungalows, one of which was occupied by Nurse Cox and in 1950 my grandmother, Maud Humphrey, became the first tenant of number 28, which was the bungalow nearest The Green on the opposite side of the estate and where I became a regular visitor especially after she retired in 1956. She had left the cottage at 23 Bedford Road, which I think was still without a bathroom and still used a communal row of outside lavatories. Even this long after the war she still had to notify the authorities of her change of address so that her National Registration Identity Card could be amended. It was an offence to fail to carry the card or produce it to a police officer or member of the armed forces on duty. The cards didn't have a photograph and seem now to have been fairly easy to forge but they remained compulsory until 1952.

Gran Maud's new bungalow, 28 Woodlands Avenue

Gran Maud distributes safety spectacles at AC-Delco not long before she retired. [photo: AC-Delco Ltd]

Following The Green round, from Gran Maud's bungalow there was an area of woodland, part of Houghton Hall estate, before you came to the entrances to the stables, the kitchen gardens and the lodge belonging to the Hall and eventually the main gates of Houghton Hall itself. Maud soon became friendly with most of the outside and domestic staff at the Hall and it wasn't long before I was helping her to modify a section of the chain-link fence at the bottom of her garden so that it could be rolled back to give her access to the woods and through to the game and poultry pens and the kitchen gardens beyond. I often used to accompany her and by the time I was a teenager I had virtually free access to the whole of the estate and grounds on my own. In the woods around the Hall there were regular culls of rooks and pigeons and Maud always obtained a supply to add to our food supply. Only the breasts were used from the rooks and these were mixed with a few vegetables and a little bacon and made into pies. The pigeons could be plucked and roasted whole like chickens, but again were more likely to be made into pies.

Mr Lewis was the gardener and he lived within the grounds with his wife who I think assisted both in the gardens and in the big house. He had really round cheeks that were as rosy as an apple and I remember that, in common with many that worked on the land, his ruddy weather-beaten face was in stark contrast to an almost pure white forehead on the rare occasions he took his cap off. Some lovely produce was grown in the walled garden and I remember the appetising smells of tomatoes ripening in the huge lean-to green house and of stored apples and onions in other outbuildings. Needless to say, Maud never went short when fruit and vegetables were in season, and my favourite memory of the

Hall is of eating strawberries straight from the bed as I picked more to take back to Gran Maud's to have sprinkled with sugar and covered in evaporated milk.

Houghton Hall was the home of Lt. Col. (later Sir) Dealtry Charles Part and his wife. They also had an estate in Scotland and it was during their visits there that I was able to get into the Hall with Gran Maud and see how the other half lived. It would have suited me fine and I felt totally at home in the 'big house' sitting in an armchair looking out over the terrace and gardens to the ha-ha and parkland beyond. I remember 'the Colonel', as he was always known, taking the salute at the Remembrance Day parade and, when I was at the school on the green, it was a regular sight to see him being driven out from the Hall, along the road that almost split the Green in two, by his chauffeur Mr Parker. I first remember him having an old limousine of some sort but then he got a brand new car – a silver Triumph Mayflower known as the razor-edge because of its sharp square lines. It was only a small car and even then it seemed odd to see one being driven by a uniformed chauffeur. A number of years later exactly the same model but in dark blue became my first car, but I had to drive it myself.

The Colonel kept race horses in training and his popularity in the village was probably at it highest when one of his horses called Falls of Shin had a long run of success, with many of the local population including Uncle Joe backing it and making a tidy profit. Joe and his drinking mates in the Kings Arms used to call it Falls of something else beginning with Sh. But the horse did them proud for at least a couple of seasons. The Colonel died in February 1961 and Lady Part was around for a good while afterwards but had gone a bit senile some time before then. If she came across you in the grounds her favourite challenge was 'I say. Who are you? Where do you come from?' It was always easier to keep walking than to try and explain that you had permission really. In the later years, Maud was often asked to make sure her hair was combed, that she didn't have odd stockings on and that she was wearing knickers before she went somewhere important.

To the right of the main gate the Hall's red brick boundary wall swept round in a curve and alongside it, running off the Green, was a wide track that followed the estate boundary round past where the wall became a wooden fence. Beyond the fence was the strip of woodland that followed most of the boundaries of the Houghton Hall estate and it was in this area of the woods that I would often stroll and remember there being a plant like a giant rhubarb that grew more than twelve feet high. Off the track was the public footpath that joined up with others and led to Dog Kennel Walk next to Dunstable Grammar School. Further round the Green were the buildings that housed the kennels of the Hertfordshire Hunt. The hounds were exercised regularly and sometimes the huntsmen would make the mistake of bringing them out at the same time that the school was out for play or lunch and this would lead to a mass of kids patting dogs and dogs licking kids and sometimes attempting rather more amorous activity, all of which would take ages for the men to sort out. Sometimes the hounds were taken out with horses but often the huntsmen were on foot with whips to crack to control but only very rarely hit a dog when it did something too naughty. Even when they were on foot the huntsmen still wore riding boots and breeches. The hounds were obviously trained to hunt foxes and you may imagine them to be a bit fierce, but in fact they were really sloppy animals and I never knew a child to be bitten. The hunt itself was a magnificent sight on the few occasions it actually met in the village and it will be a tragedy if the law causes such scenes to disappear from country life. Usually on hunt day, the hounds were loaded into a horsebox and driven off past the school barking madly with excitement.

Next to the kennels was Park Farm and then came my old school – Whitehead Voluntary Primary with the Headmaster's House adjoining on the Park Farm side. There was a small yard at the front of the school and Boys' and Girls' separate playgrounds at the rear, but these were normally ignored if the weather was fine and the area of the Green between the school and the road down to Houghton Hall would be our play domain. At the front, a privet hedge separated the school from the Headmaster's house. A similar hedge was later planted across the frontage of the school replacing railings, which I think had been taken away earlier as scrap to help the war effort.

During my time at the school it was Mr and Mrs Chaperlin living at the School House, but later when my sister Margaret and brother Nigel were there it was Mr and Mrs Frank Faiers who became Head when Mr Chaperlin retired in 1954. Sid Chaperlin was quite a character and I recall one story Mum told about him. She met him in the street one day and as he approached he pretended to walk like a very old man and asked Mum in a quivering voice how she was feeling now that she too was so very old. Mum was mystified until they exchanged explanations. Mum had just had a birthday and when asked by her offspring how old she was she had jokingly reversed the numbers. My sister Jennifer had duly gone to school and written in her diary 'my Mum is eighty-three today'.

Next to the school was the Red House, which was the home of

General Smythe. When he died towards the end of my time at the School on the Green, we were all taken out of school to line the pavement between the Red House and the Church as the hearse went by. I was stationed outside Tansley's fish and chip shop and carefully stood to attention and removed my cap as we had been instructed to do. The General's sister was Dame Ethel Smythe who was the first English female classical composer to become internationally famous. She was also a prominent suffragette and wrote the marching songs and anthems for the votes for women movement. Mum and Gran Maud attended the clearance sale at the house that followed the General's death and among their purchases was a dark oak bookcase, which I still have, and a leather music case that they bought for me to carry my books in my first year at grammar school. The family may have been responsible for destroying Dame Ethel's last great work because, years later, I discovered to my horror that the case had been full of papers that had been consigned to a bonfire by Maud, dismissed as 'just Dame Ethel's old scribblings'!

Next came a house with an extension that housed a very small shop run by Miss Bird. It may have sold some groceries and other things but all I remember is that it sold sweets – liquorice sticks, sherbet dabs and dips, chews, aniseed balls, black jacks at four for a penny, dolly mixtures and lemon crystals, bought by the ounce in a small paper bag and eaten by licking a finger, dipping it into the crystals and then sucking them off, leaving both finger and tongue stained bright yellow. Later Wagon Wheels became one of Jennifer's favourite purchases at a time when they really were much bigger than today's version – nearly five inches in diameter. The shop was still going when I was riding a motorbike and buying cigarettes rather than sweets.

Before heading into High Street, I shall cross the road and complete the circuit of The Green. The main road ran through rather than round The Green itself and, although the great majority of The Green was south of the road, there was still a sizeable area of grass to the north. Along this, there were a few residential buildings and then Park Avenue, a cul-de-sac of 1930s style houses. Beyond this, more houses and then set well back into the site was the original Memorial Hall, a corrugated iron building that catered for many village activities including the Women's Institute. The new Memorial Hall made of brick and much more substantial was built in front of the old hall and opened in 1957 after years of village fund raising. The old hall was retained and used among other things as the 'Mixed' Youth Club which was held on Mondays, Thursdays and Fridays from 6.15pm to 9.15pm and which, around 1960, was described in the village guide as having activities that 'included billiards, snooker, table tennis, dancing and good companionship'. I attended very occasionally, wasn't great at any of the sports and obviously didn't find the companionship all that good.

Along from the Memorial Hall frontage there was a tall red brick wall with a wooden door in it that was never opened and often left me wondering as a child what sort of 'secret garden' was behind. This adjoined Park Cottages, which formed the corner of Drury Lane. In one of these, fronting on to The Green, lived the bachelor brothers Bert and Frank Buckingham. Bert was the practical one and Francis was the artistic one I visited weekly for piano lessons. Jennifer also attended briefly but I went for some considerable time, completely wasting Mum and Dad's hard earned cash. My problem was that I found I could play by ear and

Houghton Regis W.I. pose outside the new memorial hall. Gran Maud is far-right and Mum is standing centre in the light (yellow) dress. Among those also pictured are: Mrs King, Mrs Tompkins, Mrs McWhirter, Mrs Joyce, Mrs Winnie Davies, Mrs Cawdell, Mrs Ager, Mrs Allen and Mrs Edna Dudley. [photo: Courtesy Mr Bruce Turvey]

was therefore too lazy to learn to read music properly – what was the point? Frank was too nice to sort me out and only very gently suggested that I should play what was written in the book rather than my own version of it.

Also in Park cottages lived Mrs and Mr Parker, the Chauffeur at Houghton Hall I have already mentioned. Thinking back, he actually did look a little bit like Parker who drove Miss Penelope in Thunderbirds on TV – perhaps he was the model. The other resident I remember is Mr Townsend, the Butler at the Hall, who often brought Gran Maud treats in quantities sufficient for us to share – venison and grouse when the Parts had been to their Scottish estate for example. He also brought her smaller offerings – often something delivered personally to her back door in a china basin covered with a cloth as ' a bit of supper'. He wasn't always so generous to his employers. One evening Gran Maud was in the kitchen at the Hall with Townsend and various other hangers-on after he had served dinner. Suddenly Lady Part appeared and said 'I say Townsend, that was delicious. Do you think we could have some more?' Back came the reply 'certainly not - get back in there and I'll see what's left after we've finished.'

Drury Lane consisted mostly of fairly modern houses but, near the top, there was a very old timbered cottage near which a footpath ran linking with the top of Park Avenue and running through close to All Saints Church. The Green itself made a lovely venue for the Cricket Club and was also the home of Houghton Rangers Football Club. The school sports and various fetes were held on The Green and once a year in September it saw the eagerly awaited arrival of the 'Statty' (Statute) Fair where we would invariably win two or three goldfish, one of which would possibly survive more than a few days.

10

THE HIGH STREET

More of my village tour now as my mental stroll moves on to the High Street:

The Green to the church

Leaving the Green at Miss Bird's shop and heading towards the church, the first establishment on the left side of the road was Tansley's fish and chip shop. I don't recall ever seeing Jack Tansley out of the shop or out of his white overall coat. His wife Nellie did have a life outside her white coat and cap, but on the few times I saw her in the village in 'civvies' she still carried the smell of the chip fryer with her. Mum occasionally patronised the shop when a quick meal was required and our favourite fish was gurnet (rock salmon). We kids would sometimes devote part of our pocket money to three pen'worth or even six pen'worth of chips in a small greaseproof paper bag with loads of salt and vinegar that always tasted better than the salt or vinegar at home. The chips were always wrapped in the obligatory old newspaper that turned your fingers black and gave you that distinctive taste mixture of chips and newsprint, but the most likely purchase was a pen'worth of scratchings or scrats, which were the little bits of batter that fell off the pieces of fish during frying and were collected up on a tray above the fat to drain. Nellie died aged 66 in 1964 and was one of

Gran Maud's laying out 'customers'.

Next came some iron railings with a vegetable garden behind them, and set well back from the road was Timmy Allen's knackers yard housed in a big black shed. This was far enough from the footpath to make all the activities going on there a bit mysterious. Sometimes there would be vast quantities of steam as different parts of various animals were boiled up for whatever reason. At other times you would catch a glimpse of a whole cow strung up by its rear feet on a large 'A' frame to be stripped of its hide and then butchered, but whatever the activity there was always the all pervading smell, particularly if the wind was in the wrong direction, of whatever was or had been recently boiling. Everything dealt with by Timmy was supposed to be unfit for human consumption but it was rumoured that some villagers bought cheap meat there. I wouldn't have fancied it even if he had been giving it away.

By contrast, beyond the next building was the little white painted, neat and clean shop that was F W Pratt the butcher's at 133 High Street. I remember Fred Pratt being in charge and when he retired his son Peter took over. An early memory is of joints of meat hanging on hooks – no fridge in use while the shop was open - and of the smell of the sawdust that was used on the floor behind the counter to soak up any blood spilt. Next came two pairs of semi-detached cottages, the second pair of which had four high gabled windows on the first floor and somewhat strangely had tiled porches over the ground floor windows but not over the front doors. My old primary school teacher Laura Freeman used to live in one of these.

Next, almost opposite the church was Jasper Perry's emporium. Jasper was a dapper man with sparse dark hair slicked back over his head with copious amounts of brilliantine or Brylcream. Unusually for those days he wore tinted glasses and always wore a collar and tie under the ever-present white overall coat that very often wasn't very white. You could buy just about anything in Jasper's shop from stockings to bundles of kindling wood, from cheese to paraffin and from lemonade to firelighters. Jasper was always busy, always hassled but always found time to wipe his hands down the front of his overall before serving the next selection from his vast and varied stock. Some, with fewer principles than me or, as is more likely, far less frightened than me of being caught, found Jasper's to be an ideal environment in which to serve their shoplifting apprenticeships. Further along was a baker's shop with a large Hovis sign in gold coloured letters.

Back to the Green and on the right hand side of the High Street dominating the view towards the church was the old Tithe Barn and Tithe Farmhouse. The barn was situated back from and roughly parallel with the road and was enormous, with two huge gabled entrance doors along its side, each capable of accommodating a horse and cart. Although roofed in corrugated iron painted black, the timbered walls were intact and the interior beams and roof supports were magnificent, even awe-inspiring. The barn was built around 1400, was ripe for and by no means beyond sympathetic renovation. It was nothing short of a criminal act of civic vandalism when it was demolished in 1964 to make way for the London overspill development. The farmhouse itself was built close to and along the line of the road and was a tall building with four very prominent chimneys. There were other barns and buildings associated with the farm between the house and the Tithe Barn itself. Next to Tithe Farm were two residential

137

buildings set further back from the road, the second one being 'L' shaped, and even further back was the next building which was the old National School. This was used for various church and community purposes including Sunday school. I attended Sunday school fairly briefly and it obviously had little effect, as my only memory is of making a cross out of a palm leaf to take home one Palm Sunday. Near the National School was the side entrance to the churchyard where a gate gave access to the path that ran behind the old fire station and Workhouse Row cottages to the front porch of the church. There was a surfaced footpath between the National School and the boundary wall of the churchyard that linked back to the footpaths to East Hill Lane, Grove Farm and Bidwell.

Next, surrounded by a small plantation of trees, was the old fire station. I first recall it no longer used as a fire station but still with its wooden double doors at the front and a four-paned rectangular window over them and a square glazed lamp above them both that still bore traces of the painted words Fire Station. Later the front doors and the lamp were removed and the front part of the building was converted into a bus shelter. Between here and the front entrance to the church was Workhouse Row, a long terrace of red brick cottages with walled gardens to the front and backing directly on to the churchyard. Attached as a lean-to at the fire station end of the row and better viewed from the churchyard was the old village lock up. This had a heavy studded door and in earlier times had been used to accommodate drunks, etc. overnight before being taken to court in Luton or Dunstable. It held a certain morbid fascination for us as children as we imagined what villains could have been incarcerated there or even being locked up ourselves.

Behind Workhouse Row and in an imposing position at the junction of High Street with Bedford Road stood All Saints Church and although as a family we were by no means devoted Christians it did play quite a part in my early life. Until my voice broke I was a member of the choir and usually attended both Matins and Evensong every Sunday. In addition there were fairly regular weddings for which we were paid two shillings (10p), and I remember one fantastic Saturday when we were booked for three weddings and felt very rich for a while. Less frequently we were required for funerals and, no doubt to compensate for the stress of sitting quite close to a wooden box containing something none of us had ever seen or ever really wanted to, we were paid half a crown or even three shillings. Our choirmaster was Mr Wilf Ivory whom I remember as a very kind and patient man.

I only knew two Vicars; the first was Rev Charlie Fletcher who was in post until I was ten or eleven. I remember an old lady connected with the church who always called him 'muster Fletcher'; the fact is that he was slightly mad and that his wife was slightly madder but they both seemed harmless enough. In 1952 the village saw the arrival of Rev Leslie Blackburn who was to stay for over twenty years. Les was quite a character. In his early years he upset quite a few by 'going high church' and burning incense and by not doing things the way 'muster Fletcher would have done'. In his later years he upset others by being regularly seen wandering along the High Street, cassock front covered in fag ash, reading the Racing Post or Sporting Life and having to be occasionally collected from the Kings Arms on a Saturday having gone in to refresh himself after a wedding and still being there when the next wedding was due to start.

Angelic choirboy, obviously growing out of his cassock

Stories and rumours about Les abounded. It was alleged that the only reason that a new vicarage had to be built was that the roof on the old vicarage began to leak like a sieve after Les had removed and sold most of the lead. After the old vicarage had been sold for conversion into council offices, large quantities of lead piping and other antique fittings with good re-sale value went missing and it was alleged that Les knew exactly where they had gone. It was alleged that when money was raised for missionary work in Africa it was never really possible to establish whether the cash had ever got any further than Bedford Road. I have no idea whether there was any truth in any of these stories. All I can say is that whenever we needed him, particularly when Gran Maud died, he couldn't have been kinder, more helpful or more considerate. Was he a rogue? – possibly. Was he loveable? – definitely.

I can't leave the church without recounting one of Dad's escapades. For a number of years he was a Sidesman, assisting the two Churchwardens and taking the collection plate round. For this he always had to be tidily dressed and sometimes sacrificed warmth for smartness. For two Sundays running the heating had not been working properly in the church and he had come home

140

frozen. The following Sunday he was determined not to let this happen again and under his coat he put on an old leather jerkin that he had worn for many years in the garden. Over those years it had been ripped so many times by brambles, roses, nails and other sharp objects that it hung all over in shaggy rags and tatters, but Dad had defied all mother's attempts to get rid of it. Unfortunately for him the heating had been mended – not just mended but made to work better than it had done for years - and all over the church you could see members of the congregation removing scarves, overcoats and further layers as it got warmer and warmer. But with what he had on underneath Dad just daren't take his topcoat off and got hotter and hotter as the service went on and was giving an excellent impression of a soggy beetroot by the time he finally escaped.

Mention of the church heating reminds me of another village

High Street looking west
[Photo: Wm Henry Cox, Courtesy of Houghton Regis Town Council]

character, Lol Bright. I suppose he was the Sexton at the church doing the grave digging, tending the boilers and any other odd jobs required. As a child I remember him suddenly appearing from the bowels of the boiler room seemingly every time you passed through the churchyard. No matter the weather, he always seemed to be wearing Wellington boots and a filthy fawn Macintosh tied up with string round the waist and always had half a cigarette dangling from the corner of his mouth. He had one leg considerably shorter than the other and therefore waddled from side to side as he walked. This peculiar gait, coupled with parent's warnings to stay away from him because he was 'dirty', added to his fascination. When I was older I discovered that he did have other clothes and scrubbed up reasonably well when he caught the bus to Dunstable some evenings. As far as I am aware he was fairly harmless, with Lol's only sin being the 'girlie' magazines that one of the braver lads once found in his den in the church boiler room.

The Church to Townsend Terrace

The first road off to the left was King Street, which consisted almost entirely of terraced cottages. King Street led into Walkley Road, which I think was a 1930s addition. Next off the High Street came Albert Road and then Cumberland Street. The tops of King Street, Albert Road and Cumberland Street were linked by Queens Street, which ran parallel to High Street. All this area was basically residential but Percy Ward's bakery was in Queens Street and although he normally delivered to The Hyde we did occasionally visit the bakery. I can still recall that wonderful smell of fresh baked bread and all the different types of loaves and cakes he used to bake. Percy was one of the few people I knew who had a car in the very early days and I remember being given a ride to

Luton with Dad in Percy's brand new Standard Vanguard, which was enormous for the time and had a very curved rear end.

On the corner of Cumberland Street and High Street with entrances onto both was the White Horse pub. Uncle Joe was an occasional customer and I called in a few times when I was (nearly) old enough. It was a bit dark and gloomy, with an apparently endless game of dominoes in progress and lots of men in flat caps. On the other corner of Cumberland Street was Jack Tomkins' butcher's shop. We were 'registered' here rather than with F W Pratt's when meat was rationed during and after the war. Almost next-door was Miss Shaw's Surgery, a mysterious square shaped building in which the curtains were always closed. Miss Shaw helped her father run the grocer's shop almost opposite and was also a registered nurse. When the grocer's shop closed for lunch or was quiet, she would open up her surgery to deal with any patients requiring her services. I think her name was Winifred (Win) but, when she made her regular visits to the school on the green to conduct head inspections (literally with a fine tooth comb made of steel), she was always known as 'Nitty Norah, flea explorer'.

A row of residential properties followed, including some with high gabled windows, until you came to the Five Bells, a white painted building that stood slightly nearer the road than properties either side of it. Again I was an occasional customer in what was usually a clean and tidy pub. Next came Ken Dickens' sweet shop, Mr Baughan's cycle shop and then a tiny grocery shop on the end of a terrace of cottages, which was run by Mrs Timms. Mr Baughan was a tall man with the permanent stooped shoulders that many cyclists seem to have, and I believe I remember a moustache. He was always busy working on cycles in the shop but could break off from whatever he was doing and immediately lay hands on the precise bike bit you were looking for. Beyond Baughan's there was a row of terraced cottages and more residential properties until you got to Townsend Farm, at which point the road turned sharp left towards the cement works and Dunstable.

Let's go back to the church and look at the other side of the High Street. The first building on the corner of Bedford Road was the Kings Arms selling Benskins Ales. This was the largest and most modern pub in the village, having been built just before the war to replace an earlier building of the same name. It was where Uncle Joe and Aunty Gert were fairly regular customers. Jennifer and I would often hang around outside on a summer evening until someone eventually told Joe we were there and he would duly oblige with a packet of Smiths crisps and a lemonade or better still a weak shandy. Beyond the Kings Arms the buildings were mostly residential and included some of the oldest houses in the village. I only remember five or six businesses on this side of the street.

Mr Shaw's grocery shop is the most memorable. Known as 'Pop' and with white hair surrounding a shiny bald pate, Mr Shaw ran the shop with his daughter. The mixture of appetising smells in the shop was amazing, and the most memorable feature compared to today is the lack of packaging. Almost everything came loose and was weighed and placed in brown paper bags or cones made by rolling sheets of thick blue paper and with greaseproof paper being used for things like bacon, cheese and butter. Prunes, sultanas and currants came in large wooden boxes; sugar and flour came in sacks; cheese came in whole or part cheeses and was cut with a wire; sides of bacon hung from hooks and were sliced to order. The floor of the shop consisted of plain boards, regularly swept, and the counters were mahogany with marble slabs to keep some stock cool. Even at the height of rationing when things were often short, the shop was always an Aladdin's cave of food with real tastes and real aromas. It would be great to travel back in time and to be let loose with a very large shopping bag!

Further up the street was Johnnie Odman's newsagent's shop. I was never a lover of that part of the day before 10am, so I didn't become one of Johnnie's army of delivery boys, but I did call in to the shop occasionally. Shop is an exaggeration, as all that was there was a counter behind which Johnnie was to be found seemingly always either undoing or tying up a stack of newspapers with hairy string. On display was a meagre selection of cigarettes and a few magazines with curly edges. I recall Johnnie being fairly small, with spectacles and always a cap and very often wearing an overcoat and fingerless gloves, as any form of heating in the building seemed to be an unnecessary luxury.

Also in this area was the barber's shop run by Cliff Sinfield where I was taken for a 'short back and sides' from an early age. Cliff could well have been the inspiration for the old story about the young man who went into the barber's and asked for a Tony Curtis. The barber snipped away and then showed him the results in the mirror. The young man was horrified and said, 'Tony Curtis doesn't have his hair done like that.' To which the barber instantly replied, 'he would if he came here.' As soon as I started work or perhaps even before, I escaped to more stylish salons in Dunstable or Luton that offered blow waves and knew their DAs (Dickie Attenborough or Duck's Arse) from their elbows. To Cliff's eternal credit, though, he made many young men feel very grown up when he asked them for the first time whether they needed 'something for the weekend'. Ronald Clifford Sinfield died young and was only 53 when he joined Gran Maud's list of customers in 1961.

Towards the top of the street on this side was a garage and Esso filling station that people often called Pratt's garage after a previous owner, but was then trading as H A Tompkins' and was actually run by Mr A A Hobbs. Also somewhere in this area was a tiny cobbler's shop run by W T 'Billy' Higgs whom I remember as shortish and very round and combining his shoe repairs with being the school crossing patrol for the County Primary School. I think he died around 1957. It was also on this side of the High Street that Ben Tompkins and before him his father Percy had their painter and decorator's yard attached to their home. Ben often did work at The Hyde and pushed all his ladders, wallpapers and paints on a handcart. The county primary – 'top school' - was the last building in High Street, with Townsend Farm opposite as the road curved. Off the bend was Mill Road, which had a small number of houses before it became an unmade lane leading to the corn mill. The mill was still there but minus its sails and was surrounded by an enormous field usually planted with cereals. Beyond the mill the path led to Blue Waters, which were disused chalk workings much older than the cement works pits, surrounded by pretty bushes and reeds and full of the deep blue water that gave the area its name. It was no doubt dangerous, was declared out of bounds unless accompanied by an adult and was therefore totally irresistible. I spent many happy hours there and fortunately lived to tell the tale. Round the bend came Townsend Terrace, a row of houses built on a fairly high bank, and then nothing but fields and the chalk pits worked by the cement works.

11

VILLAGE BITS AND PIECES

In this chapter I intend to describe some parts of the village I haven't covered previously and some more characters that were part of everyday life in Houghton Regis when I was a lad.

Bedford Road and Bidwell

As you turned from High Street into Bedford Road, the church was on your right and the Kings Arms on your left. Next on the left was an area known as the Cock Yard by virtue of the fact that a pub or beer-house of this name was once situated there. Then came the sweet shop owned by Mr and Mrs George of which I have fond memories. You climbed up steps to the front door that was actually on the side of the building and a bell clanged as the door opened. On the counter was some form of soda fountain that included a huge glass sphere containing a brightly coloured liquid that could be red, green or yellow and from which were dispensed 'penny drinks'. They all seemed to taste the same no matter what colour they were, were all sickly sweet and would probably be classified as totally unhealthy or even toxic nowadays. Although the war had ended in 1945, sweets didn't finally come off ration until February 1953, so there were careful choices to be made from what could be a very limited stock to make up your four-ounce ration for the week. Cigarettes were also hard to come by and Mr George used to try to make sure that his regulars – including Mum - always had a supply of some sort. She preferred Players or Senior Service if she could get them, but often Mr George would produce all sorts of weird brands from under the counter for me to take home for her including American Chesterfield and Camel, English Black Cat, Craven A and Kensitas and Turkish Abdullah.

Before continuing the tour, perhaps I should explain a bit about rationing. It started during the war and carried on long afterwards. What was 'on' and what was 'off' varied from time to time as did the amounts allowed. Everyone had a ration book from which coupons were cut out or allowances marked off by the supplier as they were received with indelible pencil or crayon. Children had slightly different allowances, pregnant women had special green books that allowed them more of certain things and mothers who were breastfeeding were allowed extra milk. In 1948, three years after the war had ended, the adult allowances of main foods were as follows:

per week:	butter or margarine	7oz
	lard or dripping	2oz
	sugar	8oz
	tea	2oz
	sweets	4oz
	cheese	1.5oz
	milk	3 pints
	meat	1 shillings worth
per fortnight:	bacon or ham	2oz
when available:	eggs	1 egg per book

After the war things took a long time to get back to normal and items came off ration as follows:

1948	flour
1949	clothes
1950	canned fruit, dried fruit, chocolate biscuits, treacle, syrup, jellies, mincemeat, spam and petrol
1952	tea
1953	sweets

Another effect of rationing and shortages was that supplies of some items were only available near where they were manufactured. An example was breakfast cereals. We could normally only get Welgar Shredded Wheat and Farmers Glory Cornflakes, as shredded wheat was made not far away at Welwyn Garden City (hence the brand name) and the cornflakes were probably also locally produced. It was a real treat therefore when we took a very long bus ride to visit a family friend, Mrs Cottingham, who had moved to Thrapston, and came back with a large box of Weetabix, which was made nearby in Burton Latimer.

Anyway, back to Bedford Road. Still on the left, there were a few houses before you came to a much larger house set back from the road with bay windows and silver painted wrought ironwork decorating the building. This was the home of Mr and Mrs Brian Goosey of A B Goosey Ltd Constructional Engineers who specialised in fabricating and erecting steel framed buildings. I believe Gran Maud had done some night nursing for Brian's mother and we seemed to know the family fairly well. There was a son,

Michael, about my age who I think went to private school. Next came a detached house that always seemed dark and foreboding where someone called Lizzie had once lived, and then came St Michaels Avenue. On the other side of the road, after the church came the vicarage (and later the new vicarage), and then almost opposite the entrance to St Michaels Avenue was the gate to the church allotments known as Churchfields.

St Michaels Avenue was then only a fairly short cul-de-sac and ended at the tarmac footpath that linked High Street with the Bidwell Hill council housing estate. Aunty Gert and Uncle Joe lived at number 2, a detached house that was the first on the right. I was a fairly frequent visitor, especially if pocket money was running short or in later years if a loan was required to help with the purchase or repair of a motorcycle. In the back garden there was a large shed that contained an almost unheard of luxury – a washing machine. This was probably a throwback to the time that the whole family used to 'take in washing' (in other words, do other people's laundry) to earn a few shillings. The machine was basically a large tub shaped electric boiler with a huge paddle agitator that moved the clothes back and forwards and an attached powered mangle that could easily take your fingers with the clothes. It dwarfed the little Hoover machine that Mum eventually got and as a child I could happily watch it for ages. I can still recall the smells of the Lux soapflakes, the washing soda crystals, the Robin starch (for stiffening cuffs and collars) and blue bags (for making whites whiter) and hot sheets being mangled on one of Gert's washing days.

The Churchfields allotments were pretty well sought after and by the time of the compulsory purchase order for the land for development in 1957 there were sixty-six allotment holders on land covering just over twelve acres. Gran Maud had one just inside the gate for years and I believe she was for a long time the only woman to hold an allotment on the site, but by 1957 she had given hers up to George Germaine (Uncle Joe) and there were by then two other female tenants. With this allotment and with land also under cultivation at The Hyde and Maud's own house, the family certainly did its bit for the wartime 'Dig for Victory' campaign and we were certainly never short of vegetables.

Maud didn't have far to go to get to her allotment, as the row of cottages where Mum was born was just across the road and just beyond St Michaels Avenue. There were six cottages in the row, which was situated on a bank above the level of the road. All had steps up to a front door from the pavement but the front doors were rarely if ever used. Access was usually via a path on the St Michaels Avenue side of the row that passed the block of toilets used by the whole row. All the cottages had an enclosed rear garden but there was free access along to all the back doors. Maud's aunt, Minnie Dickens, who was the sister of Maud's father George Humphrey and was known as 'Minnie Dinnie', had occupied the first cottage but I am not sure whether I can actually remember her. Maud lived with her mother Lizzie Humphrey at the second cottage, which was number 23 Bedford Road. Maud's half-sister Alice, who was Lizzie's daughter by her first husband John Cook, lived at the end cottage with her husband George Hunt. The houses were very basic but cosy. There was a cellar with an earth floor for coal, wood and other storage and a very distinctive smell – probably a mixture of damp and coal-dust. There was a coal fire in the front room, which had a very springy wooden floor being over the cellar area. There was no inside lavatory, no bathroom and the 'backhouse' had only a large sink and a brick-built copper boiler for heating water for washing clothes.

As you started to descend Bidwell Hill, the council housing estate was high on the left, and towards the bottom of the hill there were two or three houses or bungalows. In one of the bungalows lived

Uncle George Hunt at his back door in Bedford Road

one of Mum's best friends, Joyce Chant, and her husband Alf. Their children Hazel and Robin were older and son Micky was about the same age as me. I remember Robin playing football for Bidwell. Joyce moved away from the village after Alf died but Mum kept in touch for many years. From a young age I recall Alf being a regular but infrequent visitor to The Hyde whenever a plumber was required. He was a bear of a man who seemed always to wear blue overalls that smelled of 'plumber's hemp' and 'jointing' and was always cheerful despite often having to squeeze his large frame into spaces not designed to fit him as he tried to get at the offending bit of pipe-work.

At the bottom of the hill on the right was a house called Dell Mount where Gran Maud had worked as a young woman for a family called O'Neill and which was said to be home to several ghosts. It certainly looked the part and as children we never lingered too long in that vicinity. Nearby, on the opposite side of the road, was a place where I lingered much longer in later life. During the period that I was living away and coming back to visit Mum, Dad and the rest of the family, the Old Red Lion had become Dad's pub of choice and we spent a number of happy evenings there, including one when we all suddenly had to become 'staff' and help by washing glasses when the police visited during a late 'lock-in'. Beyond the Red Lion, Bidwell comprised no more than a couple of farms, a few cottages and some very pretty spinneys where we gathered bluebells as kids before you came to Calcutt Farm and the road started to climb up Lord's Hill towards Toddington.

South of High Street

This area has changed considerably and my memory is straining to recall precise details, but King Street ran from High Street to Queens Street and then became Walkley Road. Cumberland Street also started at the High Street and ran to Queens Street but carried on a bit further beyond there and it was off this end of Cumberland Street that Manor Park was developed in the 1950s. At some point near the Baptist Chapel Cumberland Street had a right hand link to Cemetery Road and on this road at the end of the cemetery itself there was a further right hand offshoot, which led to the main footpath to Dog Kennel Walk, Dunstable. We knew this area as Malmsey. My schoolmate John Woollison lived somewhere near here as did a real village character Mr V Bozier, known to everyone as 'Old bo jer'. He had a smallholding and a few pigs and I first remember him driving round the village in a horse and trap with a big metal tub on the back to collect waste food as 'pig swill'. He then graduated to an ancient Fordson tractor and then to a Field Marshall tractor, which was a single cylinder diesel with a huge exhaust and a very distinctive slow 'poomph poomph' sound. It was supposed to be started with a cartridge, but old Bozier couldn't be bothered with that expense and made his own explosion with paraffin and rags.

Old Bozier had been around forever – he had been a member of the village fire brigade when it still had a horse-drawn fire engine - but he shouldn't really have been around as long as he actually was. He was working one day cutting timber with his circular saw, which was a huge contraption worked off a series of belts from his tractor, when without warning the saw blade flew off and hit him clean on the head. It would have killed most men outright and the future was doubtful for a while even for him. But he survived and was soon back on his normal rounds, being a source of even more curiosity as everyone tried to catch a glimpse of the huge dent in his forehead and his redesigned moustache that now only grew on one side of his upper lip.

Alongside the Baptist Church was the sports field owned by APCM Ltd (Associated Portland Cement Manufacturers Limited), makers of Blue Circle cement and vast quantities of environment-polluting dust. The sports field was used by the cement works' own teams and was the venue for an annual sports and family day. Beyond this was the pasture field belonging to Townsend Farm and then came the cement works itself. The plant covered the whole area from Townsend Farm to Douglas Crescent, with two entrance gates set in a high wall running the whole of this length and made of (what else but?) prefabricated concrete. At the heart of the plant were huge rotating cylinders, that somehow turned chalk into cement, and a chimney (later two) that churned out thick white smoke apparently continuously. There was a row of tall silos and various other buildings associated with the manufacture and packaging of the product. Cement was transported by road in paper sacks and later also in bulk road tankers. The whole vehicle fleet was painted bright yellow with blue lettering and was a very familiar sight in the area. The plant also had its own rail link.

On the opposite side of the road from near Townsend Terrace almost to the boundaries of Northfields Secondary Modern School were the quarries where chalk was extracted. Originally I remember the chalk being dug out after occasional blasting with explosives by two very large shovels on caterpillar tracks that I think were electrically powered and made a loud groaning-type noise when in operation. They could be heard from a long distance, even at The Hyde, when the wind was in the right direction and were referred to locally as 'navvies'. The chalk was then transported in huge rectangular shaped buckets run like cable cars high over the road to the plant. Later the part of the quarry nearest the road was worked-out and chalk came from workings further away from the road and was transported on a continuous conveyor belt. Lumps of chalk occasionally fell off the buckets and you always kept an eye skywards when cycling underneath. Between the road and the quarry edge there was a scrappy hawthorn hedge that was always white with dust, as were the road and footpaths unless there had been heavy rain. The whole of the cement works end of the village was usually covered in white dust. We weren't so badly affected at The Hyde but even there Mum wouldn't hang out washing if the wind was blowing in the wrong direction. If there was an inversion and the smoke from the chimney hung close to the ground there was in addition to the smoke and dust a really horrendous smell. None of this could possibly have been healthy but I was never actually aware of any health problems caused to those working at the cement works or to the general population of the village.

I have mentioned Alf Chant as a visitor to The Hyde supplementing his regular job with a little moonlighting as a plumber, but there were other regular visitors as tradesmen called or delivered much more often in those days. Ben Tompkins was our interior and exterior decorator. He was a quiet man who did an excellent job without ever rushing and I remember being fascinated watching him 'grain and varnish' the front door. The door was obviously plain softwood and the object was to get it looking like much more expensive hardwood. First there would be careful preparation and sanding and the application of 'knotting' and other mysterious potions before a strange brown liquid was applied. While still wet this was 'combed' in wavy lines and swirls with various pieces of cardboard with 'teeth' cut by Ben in different sizes. The liquid was darkish and where the 'teeth' passed through it became lighter and if done by an expert like Ben the end result would give the appearance of a nicely grained surface. This would then receive several coats of varnish and give you a door that looked good and lasted for many years.

Re-decorating inside was a winter job and after stripping the old wallpaper and filling cracks with plaster mixed from powder (no Polyfilla then) the first job would be to paint the ceiling with two coats of distemper (no emulsion paint either). The walls would then be painted with size before Ben cut the wallpaper with the biggest pair of scissors I had ever seen and expertly pasted it in place. As I said, emulsion paint didn't exist, so the kitchen and bathroom had gloss paint on the walls and with the wonderfully toxic high lead content the new paint had a lovely aroma that lasted for days despite Mum leaving halves of onions all over the place to 'take the smell'. All woodwork had an undercoat before the gloss, and if any wood was new or bare it had a primer first that was a beautiful pink colour.

Eventually either Ben became too expensive or there was less money around and Mum decided that, having carefully watched him for years and picked up various tips from him, she would take on the interior herself. She soon became quite expert and I shall never forget the look on Dad's face when he came home from work one day to find that not only had Mum stripped the wallpaper from the living room, she had also taken his crowbar to the wooden picture rails that she had decided were 'old fashioned', leaving huge holes in the walls. They were soon neatly filled and a very professional job completed. Dad's attempts to take over the exterior were adequate but not such a smooth operation. One day he was up the ladder painting a back bedroom windowsill and couldn't quite reach the last little bit. Far too much trouble to go all the way back down to the ground to move the ladder; much easier just to bounce it across a little bit. The end result was totally predictable with ladder, Dad and paint pot descending rapidly to the ground. There was no serious injury and Mum as usual laughed loud and long at her husband's misfortune until she realised that most of the paint had actually landed on Jennifer, ruining her dress and giving Mum several happy hours of removing green gloss from delicate young skin and cutting out paint-matted hair.

Other regular visitors were those delivering and selling various commodities. Percy Ward delivered the bread and occasional treats such as doughnuts smothered in sugar and oozing red jam. His bread was always unsliced and there was a choice of shapes and sizes of loaf. We normally had a flat tin loaf that gave an almost square slice but occasionally had a corrugated cylindrical loaf that gave you a perfectly round slice. There was always a nice crust and I loved it when part of the crust was a bit overdone and almost black. I think Percy originally came from his bakery in Queens Street on a tradesman's bike with a large carrier at the front. Later he came in a van but always came to the door with the bread and cakes in a large rectangular wicker basket hung over his arm. This basket became his downfall in later years. By then we had a dog that was a first cross between a German shepherd bitch and a fox terrier dog (he must have stood on a box!) and, when Robbie was a puppy, Percy used to tease him with his basket. When Robbie grew up he became just like a miniature Alsatian with perfect markings and moles but with a tail that went up instead of down. He also became a dog that would let anyone into the house but nobody out – except for Percy who he wouldn't even let past the gate once he saw that basket. Poor old Percy would stand at the gate shouting to Mum to get the dog in before he dared venture up the drive.

Percy brought the bread but I have no idea who brought the milk because I was never up early enough to see him. I do know though that it wasn't Mr Inward. Mr Inward was a milkman who delivered around the village from the back of an old ex-RAF pick up truck. He always wore a brown overall coat with an overcoat or Mac over the top in the wintertime, a leather cash bag like a bus conductor's used to hang over his shoulder and there was always a trilby hat perched on the back of his head. Unlike other milkmen he didn't seem to start his deliveries until the afternoon, and in the winter was often still on his rounds when it got dark, hence his nickname 'the midnight milkman'. Another caller was the 'pop man' who brought to the door Corona lemonade, Tizer and Smiths Crisps. A real treat was Tizer with a dollop of ice cream in it, and sometimes for a change we had dandelion and burdock or cream soda to drink. There were also regular visits from the men from Kleeneze and Bettawear who both sold wide ranges of brushes and polishes but unlike today they didn't produce a catalogue and take your order for later delivery; they carried a huge suitcase crammed with at least one of everything they sold and several of the more popular items. Only if they didn't have what you wanted with them would they come back another day with it. Mum regularly bought Kleeneze products and thought their furniture polish was by far the best, but she occasionally bought something from the Bettawear man because she felt sorry for him.

Another caller very unusual for the time and for us children actually a bit frightening because we had never seen the like before, was a Sikh with full beard and turban who also carted round an enormous and heavy suitcase. He was selling ties, scarves and fabrics that were all far more colourful and in some cases better quality than was available in the shops. Mum bought a few items from time to time and always gave him a cup of tea. He was invariably very grateful, as no doubt he would almost certainly have been turned away from many places because of his colour. But for being frightening nobody could beat the coal man. In the early days the coal still came by horse and cart and was carried in sacks into a coal store that was built into the house alongside an outside lavatory and could hold at least a ton and a half of coal. The cart was pulled by two huge shire horses and was driven by a man whose surname I think was Hines but was known universally as 'Pegleg' for the very good reason that he had an artificial leg that was just that – a peg of wood.

From the road to the coal shed was a long way for a man with two legs, never mind one, so Pegleg would always insist on opening up the double gates and driving the cart and horses up the drive. Having a large cart pulled by two huge horses stamping their hooves and snorting hot steamy breath literally right outside your back door was bad enough, but the rig being driven by the driver from hell was something else. A large man, black with coal dust with either a bandana or a strange round leather hat on a head covered in long dirty hair, wearing a jerkin with a heavy leather back to protect him from the sacks and shiny pieces of leather sheathing his forearms, a pair of trousers tied with string below the knee to reveal one hobnailed boot and one piece of wood with a round knob on the end. Add to this shouted commands to the horses, with every second word being a swear word, and you begin to get the picture, but the real performance was yet to come. Knackered from humping twenty sacks of wet coal off the cart and into the shed and without room to turn round, Pegleg then had the task or persuading the horses to reverse down a drive with more than a slight curve in it and back through the gates onto the road. Fascination always overcame fear and I very often learnt a new word or two.

12

WEATHERMAN

When I left school in July 1957 jobs were plentiful – it wasn't a question of could I get a job but more which job would I like. The head of AC-Delco apprentice school, I think he was called Jim Cross, actually came and saw me at home and spent a long time trying to persuade me to apply for an apprenticeship at Delco. John Bright, the son of Fred and Kate Bright who lived on Bidwell Hill and were friends of the family, also came to visit and chatted to me about working for SKF Bearings in Luton and someone else was pushing Bagshawe's in Dunstable. Uncle Ron said that he could get me into Waterlow's where he was a printer, and various other options were put forward including some rather sketchy information from 'Waddy' Wadsworth, the teacher lumbered with careers advice at Dunstable Grammar School.

I knew that Dad thought that having gone to grammar school I shouldn't have to 'get my hands dirty' to earn a living, and to be honest I didn't have any great skills at making or mending anything and the thought of working in a factory didn't really appeal that much. I gave careful consideration (for about a minute) to the possibility of staying on in the 6th form at school and also looked at becoming a junior reporter for the local press or working in a bank (there were vacancies at the Dunstable Gazette and the Luton News, and Lloyds Bank, Trustee Savings Bank and National Provincial Bank all wanted staff). In the end, though, mainly because I liked Geography and because it seemed a lot less boring than a factory, bank or large office, I eventually settled on what was then the Air Ministry Meteorological Office, which just happened to have its national operational headquarters in Dunstable. It turned out to be a very good choice.

To be pedantic, until the boundary changes of 1961 the Met Office was actually in Houghton Regis, being located between Drovers Way and the old green lane leading to Maiden's Bower near the end of Brewer's Hill Road. I don't remember an interview but I suppose I must have had one and eventually a letter arrived confirming an offer of appointment as a Scientific Assistant at a starting salary of £315pa – over £6 a week, which was good money as lads going into the factories were on about £4 and girls going to Woolworths were getting no more than £3. I would start on 28 October and after a few days at Dunstable would be off to the training centre at Stanmore in Middlesex; quite an adventure for someone who had never been further than Luton on his own. Obviously feeling lucky, I invested in the newly launched Premium Bonds. I bought just one on the basis that one was all you needed to win your fortune. I'm still waiting.

The previous year of 1956 had not been a good one, as great swathes of the village – 200 acres that included The Hyde - had been made the subject of a Compulsory Purchase Order by Luton Rural District Council to enable a massive London overspill development. Houghton Regis would be changing forever and we as a family seemed certain to be made homeless. Mum and Dad must have been worried sick, but to their credit carried on life as normally as possible for us kids as they prepared to fight their case at a public inquiry.

The threat of the Compulsory Purchase Order hung over us for well over twelve months and I was sitting at the breakfast table at the beginning of September 1957 when the postman dropped the long-anticipated, large brown envelope through the letter box. It was the Inquiry Inspector's report and Mum's fingers were trembling as she opened it. Reading the letter she went very quiet and deathly white and I feared the worst, but suddenly after a long time she started laughing slightly hysterically and saying 'we're all right. It's OK.' Having since looked at the actual bundle of papers it must have been a terrible experience reading them when your home and your whole way of life was at risk, because the first information given was that the Minister had confirmed the Order. Only if you looked at the small print carefully did you see that it had been confirmed in a modified form and only at the end did it become obvious that the modification was that three small pieces of land had been excluded – Firbanks, which was Mr Birchley's market garden of about 2 acres near Drury Lane, about 2 acres of land belonging to the church to be used to extend the All Saints churchyard and, last but not least, The Hyde. So 1957 became a year to celebrate – I had a job, we all still had a home, the new village memorial hall had finally been opened and to cap it all the Russians had launched a dog into space.

I recall very little about training in Stanmore. I shared digs in Kenton with a lad from Anglesey called Griff, whose full name was something like Owen Griffith Owen and who came from somewhere totally unpronounceable on the island, and another boy who was so memorable that I can remember absolutely nothing about him. We felt quite grown up as we travelled on the tube every day to Stanmore and back, went up to the West End a couple of times and got fairly drunk most nights. One particular night we were well over the top and had great fun pushing each other into people's front gardens on the way home. I felt quite guilty next morning as we walked to the underground station past several scenes of apparent devastation in what had been neatly trimmed privet hedges but they soon sprang back into shape. The other memory was after five years of monastic seclusion in an all male grammar school being suddenly surrounded by GIRLS. It took some getting used to and the downside was that the one that was really interested in me was certainly no raving beauty and had the worst case of halitosis I have ever come across before or since. The training centre was located in a group of former RAF buildings. We must have been taught how to 'plot' weather charts and a few basics of meteorology, but the only thing I can remember clearly is learning how to inflate and launch a weather balloon, which somewhat ironically is the one thing I never actually got to do operationally.

My posting after training was back to Dunstable, which was expected, and to MO12, one of the two main research departments, which meant normal working hours rather than shift work, which was a bonus. MO12 and MO11 were housed in a building separate from the main operational departments and adjoining the field full of radio masts and equipment that covered the greater part of the Dunstable site. The building was rather grandly named the Napier Shaw Laboratory but was really not much more than a collection of inter-connecting huts but with a fairly posh brick-built entrance. The hierarchy was fairly simple – there were scientists (Scientific

Officers of various grades) who had specific research projects to pursue; then there were lesser scientists (Experimental Officers of various grades) who assisted the scientists or had their own more minor projects, and finally there were us minions (Scientific Assistants) who just did what we were told. Research was synoptic (current weather) or climatic (longer term weather trends) and what most of the scientists were trying to do was to forecast by statistical analysis of historical weather records – find a magic formula that said if the weather is doing this and that now it is likely to change to that and this next. To help them do this much faster they would soon be getting one of the country's first computers, METEOR, but that was still a little way off when I got there, and some of the scientists were travelling regularly to use the Ferranti computer at Manchester University.

Basically, our work was extracting data from old weather reports and records and doing various calculations with the results. As ours was going to be one of the first ever computers there were obviously no personal computers or pocket calculators to help us with the statistical work but we did have some help for our brains. We had comptometers (a trade name but used for all such mechanical calculators like vacuums are all called Hoovers). These ran on mains electricity and did addition, subtraction, multiplication and simple division. We only had two of these, one of which was a Bell Plus Adder, and they were so noisy that they were kept in a small separate office called, with great originality, the computing room. You went there whenever you had any long and complicated calculations to do or whenever you wanted privacy to chat up any young lady that you just happened to know had gone in there to work. In the main office we had Burroughs machines that did addition and subtraction (sometimes with a print out like a till roll) by keying in figures and pulling the lever towards you, and for more complicated calculations we had slide rules. There was also a small, hand-held, cylindrical, stepped gear calculator called a Curta that was about the size of a coffee mug and despite being a bit fiddly had the advantage of being much quieter in use.

Initially I cycled to work or caught the bus if it was wet, but it wasn't after too many weeks of gazing longingly into the window at Ace Motorcycles in High Street North, Dunstable, that I got my own transport, became totally independent and opened up a whole new way on life. My first machine was a maroon (I think they were all the same colour) BSA B31 350cc four stroke single, registration number 235 FML. There was no restriction on engine

A Curta calculator – I've forgotten how we used them
[photo: The Calculator Reference www.v.calc.net]

size for learners in those days and it was powerful for the time and quite heavy – so heavy that after arriving home from my first excursion on the bike I had to shout for Mum to help me get it up on its stand but I soon got the hang of it. I spent many happy hours round the country lanes of Bedfordshire getting used to handling the bike (no training courses were available then) and learning how to lean it into bends and combine the front and rear wheel brakes in the right way. I had been doing this for several weeks and was out in the middle of nowhere one day when it suddenly started to rain. I had never ridden in the wet before and I had no idea how it would affect braking and leaning on corners. I was soon going to find out though as a right-angled bend was fast approaching. In the end I didn't brake enough, didn't lean over enough and found myself crossing the grass verge and riding into a ditch that was fortunately dry. It was also quite deep and I remember very clearly thinking to myself that if I didn't keep the bike going I would never get it out from there. So I managed to keep the bike trundling along the bottom of the ditch around the rest of the corner and into the straight, where eventually the ditch got shallower and I was able to ride up over the verge and back onto the road. There was not a mark on the bike and not a scratch on me but it was several minutes and at least two cigarettes later before I stopped shaking enough to carry on riding home.

It may seem strange that recalling my early days on two wheels should bring rabbits to mind but it does, because around this time myxomatosis was rife in Bedfordshire. The disease had been intentionally introduced in an attempt to reduce the rabbit population and was doubtless successful in that aim, at least initially, but the results were pathetic. Occasionally affected rabbits would find their way into the garden at The Hyde. They would have streaming, puffy eyes and swollen faces, would eventually become blind, immobile and be in obvious distress. At home I had an air rifle and could quickly put them out of their misery, but riding the country lanes on my motorcycle it became very common to find diseased rabbits in the roadway. I always felt it kindest to stop and quickly end their pain by running my rear wheel over their head and neck. So it is then that whenever I remember the pleasure of learning to use and enjoy a motorbike I always think of rabbits. I have no problem with shooting or humanely trapping them for food, but inflicting suffering by infecting them with such a horrible disease is something altogether different.

Motorcycles are very safe provided that the rider survives his first twelve months and I just about managed to do so. Once I was on the A5 Watling Street north of Dunstable and decided to overtake a lorry. It was slightly downhill and with a following wind I was probably up to my absolute maximum of almost 80mph as I began to pass, but the lorry was also speeding up on the downward slope. Suddenly there was another lorry coming in the opposite direction and all I could do was keep the throttle wide open, breathe in and hope for the best. Eventually I was through and past and a mile or so up the road I stopped for a calming smoke. It was only then that I noticed that the passing lorries had scuffed the rubber grips on my handlebars on BOTH sides. The first time I actually parted company with the bike was outside Mrs McWhirter's house in Houghton Regis as I have described in an earlier chapter, and it wasn't long after having got the bike back from repairs from that little excursion that I lost it again. I was almost home – near the entrance to Catling's farm – on the last bend before The Hyde, when I lost grip on front and rear tyres simultaneously, slid and flipped over into the ditch. I ran home half crying, half cursing that I had 'bent the bloody thing again'. Uncle Ron, rather unusually, happened to be visiting and he retrieved the bike for me. The damage was slight and, although it wasn't the last time I parted company with a bike, it was the last time that it was my fault.

I eventually took my motorcycle driving test in Luton and in those days the examiner was on foot! He just watched me ride around for a while and then told me that the next part of the test would be the emergency stop. He asked me to ride around two blocks in the centre of town in a figure of eight and at some point he would step into the road with his clipboard and signal a stop. I started to ride round and round but never saw a sign of him. After a few minutes I began to wonder if something had happened to him and whether I should go back to the test centre. There was a story going around at the time about an examiner having jumped out in front of a bike for the emergency stop and discovering too late that it was the wrong bike and that it wasn't going to stop until after it had run him down. Eventually he appeared and I did a reasonably quick stop without falling off. He wasn't happy and asked where the hell I had been. It turned out that in my nervous state I hadn't been doing a figure of eight but rather a big circle. He had been standing in the middle and of course I never passed that bit. He didn't hold it against me though and gave me the pass.

Looking back at those early days of work I must say that we had life very easy compared to today. There was always time for tea and coffee breaks in the canteen across the way. Lunch breaks were often extended with other activities such as table tennis and picnics among the radio aerials in the summer or card schools in the winter, and there was never any great pressure from the scientists for us to work too hard. We were allowed a certain number of days a year uncertified sick leave and Jock Milton our admin man even used to come round and tell us to take a day or so off if we were in danger of not using our full 'entitlement'. Most of the Scientific Assistants were young, single and many were away from home for the first time. There were frequent parties at various flats around Dunstable including one we nicknamed 'The Pit' and a lot of socialising generally. It was very much like I imagine university would have been but without the hassle of exams – and we were being paid and well paid at that for the pleasure.

Two early introductions to the social life of the office stick in my mind; At the beginning of January 1958 I was asked if I would

Party time at 'The Pit' with, left to right, Pete Ball, myself, and Jeff Bryson (standing) and Dave Calcraft, Pat Baker and John Hall (seated)

like to help out at the party held for all the children of Met Office, Dunstable, employees. One of the young girls present started showing much more interest in 'Uncle George' than was healthy for one young enough (just) to be invited to a children's party. But never one to refuse a lady I allowed her the pleasure of a little kiss and cuddle and spent the next few weeks looking over my shoulder in case her Dad had found out. At our own Christmas party held in the canteen (I think it was this same year), I had the great pleasure of being kidnapped by some members of the typing pool, being carried off to their domain and being tied to a chair from which I obviously made no attempt whatsoever to escape from their very pleasant attentions. They said I looked like pop star Marty Wilde (I suppose we both had a dimple on our chins). I would have happily stayed there all afternoon but some idiot workmate (no doubt a bit jealous) 'rescued' me.

In March 1958 my temporary appointment as a Scientific Assistant was 'confirmed', which was the first stage in the process that would hopefully see me made 'permanent' after two years service and then after passing a board eventually become 'established' as a civil servant. I began to widen my circle of friends and to become a regular at the Spread Eagle pub on the corner of Beale Street in High Street North, Dunstable, where the landlord Arthur Noon made our young and mostly ever so slightly under-aged group most welcome and served an excellent pint of Flowers Bitter. Other social events during the year included a visit to the Radio Show in London with my new mate John Hall and a party of us going to what was my first visit to the Farnborough Air Show.

On September 16th I changed motorcycles and became the

proud owner of a Zundapp 250cc two stroke 773 GMG. It turned out not to be a particularly great machine but I did achieve history with it when I picked up my first ever booking on 1st October for 'causing unnecessary obstruction' outside Luton Technical College where I was doing and very soon giving up 'A' Level Pure and Applied Mathematics. Along with the twenty or so reported at the same time, I got a written caution. Later that month I went with a party from the office on a visit to Flowers brewery in Luton to see how they made all the beer that we were beginning to drink in fairly large quantities.

When I had started work, Jennifer was only twelve, Margaret eight and Nigel six, so my fairly hectic work life and even more hectic social life meant that I missed a lot of them all growing up, especially the younger two. I do remember, though, involving them in games of football and cricket on the front lawn, often messing up Dad's hand mowed handiwork with sliding tackles or taking guard at the wicket and bashing holes in his grass with a bat. It was one of the football games that caused my first visit to hospital when I jumped over the little box hedge between the lawn and the drive, landed awkwardly and sprained my ankle. Luton and Dunstable Hospital decided that they would strap the ankle and leg up with sticky plaster and gave a little Irish nurse the task of shaving my leg. She lathered the limb and I was quite looking forward to her ministrations until she produced a huge cut-throat razor. Even that wasn't too bad until I realised that at the end of each gentle downward stroke of the blade she was giving a couple of none too delicate taps of the sharp steel edge against the skin of my ankle. I daren't say a word in case I broke her obviously deep concentration but miraculously she managed to finish without drawing blood and on the very last tap actually said 'oh I shouldn't have been doing that, should I?'

Nigel gave me the opportunity to enjoy a second childhood playing with Dinky Toys again and creating complex road and garage layouts 'for him'. I even got a bit upset whenever he decided to break up some of my creations and play with his own toys in his own way! Nigel arrived home one day from school literally covered from head to foot in liquid mud and cement mixture slurry. Asked by Mum what on earth had happened he came out with the masterly understatement 'somebody dropped a brick.' Maggie's best quote came when we had lost a cat, a large tabby cat imaginatively called 'Tabby', and some considerable time latter Maggie came staggering home with an even larger cat that she had 'found' in the village insisting that it was 'our Tabby'. When Mum explained that it couldn't be our cat because one was a mummy cat and the other was a daddy cat and that she would have to take it back, she came out with the very early display of feminine logic 'how can you expect a little girl like me to carry a big cat like that.' In the end the cat refused to go home anyway, adopted us and became, what else, 'Tubby'.

Earlier in the year I had made a return to sport, playing cricket in an inter-departmental match and consequently being asked to join the Met Office, Dunstable, team. I hadn't played cricket since school and then only during games sessions, so I had no kit and appeared in the inter-departmental friendly in ancient borrowed flannels and Dad's old boots. Although his boots were a bit small for me, I knew I would never fill them in sporting terms. As a boy he had been rescued by the Birmingham City captain, Joe Bradford, when a policeman was about to throw him out of St

Andrews for sneaking in without paying. This eventually led to him acquiring a strip for his boys club team, getting in free to matches as 'Mr Bradford's guest', becoming an occasional ball boy and helping to carry the FA Cup around the ground when Cardiff City paraded it after their 1927 Wembley victory. Later he played at quite a high level for Dunstable Athletic. In Birmingham he had been a member of the cycling section of Birchfield Harriers and thought nothing of a little 'Sunday spin' from Birmingham to the Malvern Hills and back. He played his cricket for AC-Sphinx, keeping wicket and being a handy middle order batsman. He also played water polo in freezing water storage tanks at AC and on holiday would swim considerable distances in the sea. I must have been a bit of a disappointment to him!

Anyway, back to the match; one of my bosses, Mr M K Miles was batting in the full regalia – immaculate cream flannels, sweater with club colours, a cravat, new batting gloves, his own bat and what looked suspiciously like a university 'blue' cap. The skipper asked me to bowl – something I had rarely done – and I trundled in with a couple of balls that Mr Miles met with a perfect forward defensive stroke, obviously sizing me up before hitting me out of the ground next time. I decided to try a little experiment and bowled the next one with the seam of the ball across my palm and flipped it as it left my hand. It pitched on a perfect length but then shot along the ground not bouncing higher than an inch before taking out his middle stump. Ever the gentleman, he actually said 'well bowled' through gritted teeth as he went back to the pavilion. So I was all set for 1959, which would become the year in which I played more cricket, drank more beer and went out with more girls than in any year before or since.

13

LONG HOT SUMMER

At the beginning of 1959 Luton Town started to surprise everybody, not least their faithful supporters, which included me, by starting to win FA Cup ties. I watched every home game and some of those played away as they progressed through the rounds as follows: Round 3, beat Leeds United 5-1 at home at Kenilworth Road; Round 4, beat Leicester City 4-1 in a replay after a 1-1 draw at Filbert Street; Round 5, beat Ipswich Town 5-2 away; Round 6, beat Blackpool 1-0 in a replay after drawing 1-1 at Bloomfield Road and Semi-final, beat Norwich City 1-0 at St Andrews in a replay after a 1-1 draw at White Hart Lane. I rode to the Ipswich tie at Portman Road on my Zundapp, which just about killed it off, and went by coach to both Semi-final games. With a gang from the office I had had to watch a reserve game to get vouchers for semi-final tickets and then queue at Kenilworth Road at 6am the following day to get the actual tickets. A week later, again on a Sunday, we were queuing once more for the replay tickets. By a strange coincidence, in Birmingham, the coach parked right outside the house in Witton Street where Dad had lived with his parents before moving to Dunstable. Cup fever really hit the area as can be shown by the attendances – 18,534 watched the Third round tie, 27,277 were at the replay against Leicester and by the time we played Blackpool in the Sixth round replay on 4 March I was part of the highest ever attendance at Luton of 30,069. (The capacity now is 9,975.) At least half of the 65,000 crowd at White Hart Lane were Luton fans and even for the mid-week daytime kick-off for the replay there was an attendance of 49,500.

Tickets for the Wembley final were like gold dust and, despite joining every queue and entering every raffle and competition I could find, I just couldn't get one. We still didn't have television at home, so I presume I must have watched the match at Gran Maud's. I do remember though that my mate John Hall suffered with me. Luton played Nottingham Forest, who had beaten Aston Villa in their semi, and on the big day my team just didn't perform. They had Luton's only ever England international goalkeeper in Ron Baynham, Luton's only ever Footballer of the Year (also an England international) in captain Syd Owen, Luton's all-time record holder for appearances in Bob Morton, Luton's all-time record goal scorer in Gordon Turner, a Scotland international in Alan Brown and three Irish internationals in Brendan McNally, Billy Bingham and George Cummins and were basically the team that had finished the previous season in Luton's highest ever position in the top division of the league. Despite all this and despite Nottingham Forest playing most of the match with ten men after Elton John's uncle Roy Dwight broke his leg (no substitutes allowed then), we were rubbish and lost 2-1, with poor old Bob Morton being tagged in the press as 'the only Cup Final centre forward who never had a shot at goal'.

I wrote a little piece for the Met Office sports and social club newsletter about the terrible illness called 'cup fever' and how it hadn't been possible to cure it because the cup that had been raised

Luton Town FC – FA Cup finalists in 1959. Jennifer's 'dream lover', Billy Bingham, is seated far-left

on May 2 had been decorated with the wrong colour ribbons, but I didn't realise then that I would have to wait until the 1980s before Luton's black and white colours would be tied to a cup at Wembley. It was only the Littlewood's League Cup when we beat Arsenal 2-1, but there were still tears in my eyes and memories of 1959 when Steve Foster the Hatters' skipper lifted it high. On the subject of colours I have to make a confession. The black and white scarf I wore throughout that cup run was obtained for me at trade price by one of the girls in the office, Joy Whitelam, whose father had an outfitter's shop. But that shop was up north and the scarf was a Grimsby scarf!

After Luton's defeat I consoled myself with a new motorbike

– back to a BSA B31, registration number 161 KMX that was newer than the first one and had a flashy Avon windshield that I soon made even flashier by painting white 'go faster' stripes on it. I chose a BSA because they were reliable, didn't leak too much oil and didn't need a lot of tinkering with, unlike some makes. The Japanese invasion hadn't really started and there were still large numbers of British manufacturers to choose from: AJS, Ambassador, Ariel, BSA, Cotton, Douglas, Excelsior, Francis Barnett, Greeves, Indian, James, Matchless, Norton, Panther, Royal Enfield, Sunbeam, Triumph, Velocette and Vincent each made numerous models and I could make up most of the other letters of the alphabet with some of the equally large number of European makes available in the UK: Husqvarna (Sweden), KTM (Austria), Laverda (Italy), Ossa (Spain), Universal (Switzerland) and Zundapp (Germany). Had money been no object, my choice would have been between a BSA 497cc Gold Star, a Royal Enfield Crusader or a Triumph Tiger 110.

BSA B31, 161 KMX – a loyal and (mostly) reliable friend

The cricket season was already under way and I also got involved in the new-to-me sport of Tug of War. Bill Henry was our coach and we took training very seriously, with lunchtime and evening sessions two or three times a week in the run up to competitions. We trained on a contraption designed by Bill that consisted of a series of weights and pulleys attached to one of the old radio pylons. We pulled a very heavy concrete block off the ground, lowered it down and pulled it back again numerous times, with Bill attaching more and more smaller weights to the hooks on the large block as the session progressed. At various times half of the team of six would drop out, leaving the other three to hold the block just off the ground for so many minutes before slotting back in and taking the weight back up to the top of the rig. In actual competition we would rest between pulls flat on our backs with arms and legs in the air to drain lactic acid. Bill would run around massaging leg muscles and feeding us glucose tablets to keep sugar levels high.

Our first appearance was representing Dunstable at the Met Office sports at Harrow when we beat the favourites. As far as I recall we were undefeated from then on at both Met Office and Air Ministry sports and at some local village invitation events until my last pull with the team in 1963. I didn't quite retire then, as I was in the winning team at No 5 District Police Training Centre sports day in 1964 and have a little shield to prove it. The Air Ministry sports were held at quite prestigious venues such as the University of London athletics ground at Motspur Park in Surrey and at the White City stadium in London, which was built for the 1908 Olympics and was where the AAA Championships were held for almost forty years up to 1970. It was demolished in 1984 when the BBC extended its Television Centre in Wood Lane onto it. One year at the White City I changed next to a very well known international athlete who was appearing in an invitation race – so well known that his name now escapes me but I think it may have been Bruce Tulloh.

The sports and social club newsletter that reported our first win at Harrow also mentioned one of the Met Office's real characters – Mary Galifi. Mary was a large and larger than life Irish lady with a shock of glowing red/blonde hair. She didn't just enter a room; she made an entrance. She didn't just walk; she glided. She didn't

Met. Office, Dunstable, tug-of-war team – team shirts (borrowed from a football club), boots (metal heels prohibited) and glucose tablets between pulls. I am at number two

180

just engage you in conversation; she engulfed you. Her husband was a Sicilian not much more than half her size, but somehow they were perfectly matched. The sports report read ' The sports held at Harrow were rather poorly attended by Dunstablians, but our tug of war team retrieved one of the three cups which we donated. Members of the victorious team were Messrs. S Siemsen, B Fullager, A Hall, D Bell, G Jackson and P Lindsay. Bill Henry supplied the essential lungpower and exhortations. In lighter vein, a Dunstable team became champion passers of the can, which caused no surprise, and Mary Galifi won the sack race, which did.'

The cricket season had begun with nets at the Waterlow's sports ground and carried on through a glorious summer on Wednesday evenings and Saturdays or Sundays and occasionally both. We played a few home games at the Waterlow's ground and the evening matches mostly at Bennett's Recreation Ground near Bull Pond Lane. We played teams like the Ariel Club at Eascote, Index Publishers and Bagshawe's but most of our games were out in the villages like Stanbridge, Edlesborough, Eaton Bray and Houghton Regis and even as far as Gaddesdon Row. One of our players was Bunny Deekes, who was old enough to know Mum, and even older was Wally Clemmett, who because he couldn't run was wicket keeper. Wally was a uniformed messenger at the Met Office and seemed absolutely ancient to us but was probably only in his fifties, and early in the season he did me a very good turn. We had just started to field, with Wally behind the stumps as usual, when he stretched to get to a ball and went down in a heap with a torn muscle in his leg. I just happened to be closest to the skipper and was first to volunteer to take over as soon as it became clear that Wally couldn't continue. I took a couple of catches, and to be honest it wasn't difficult to look very mobile and athletic when it was Wally that I was following, and I made the gloves mine from then on.

Other members of the team I remember from those early days were Tony Toombs, my best friend from school who had by then also joined the Met Office; Ken Saunders, a very fast and very good bowler who gave me plenty of catch victims behind the sticks; Mike Collins, a lad with bright ginger hair who was a good bowler but difficult to keep to as he bowled fast medium left arm over most of the time. Eric Hughes from Buxton in Derbyshire who was also a bowler but slightly more erratic; John Hall from Cardiff with whom I have kept in touch over the years, and Dave Calcraft, a giant of a man who was to spend many years in the Falkland Islands. Our umpire was Geoff Leaf who later briefly became one of the TV weathermen. Dave Calcraft, who used to perch astride an Ambassador two-stroke motorbike that looked tiny against his frame, once saved me a lot of money. I had come off my bike on ice, twisting the forks, and rode around for several days with handlebars pointing left when I was riding straight. Dave had a look one lunchtime, gripped the front wheel between his knees, grasped the handlebars with his shovel-like hands and just pulled the forks straight, taking a fair quantity of skin off his fingers in the process. Dave was posted to Exeter in May 1959 prior to going to the Falklands, and John, Tony and Eric became my very good mates.

John Hall had joined the Met Office in 1956 and in August 1957 came to MO11 in Dunstable from Rhoose (now more majestically known as Cardiff Wales International Airport). We became very

Pulling on the 'keeper's gloves at Bennett's Rec'. Eric Hughes, in typical hands-in-pockets stance, is in the background

close friends exchanging all sorts of confidences. John didn't (and still doesn't) drive; he was very often my pillion passenger to and from cricket matches and I remember us roaring around the country lanes singing the latest Top 20 hit at the top of our voices. I cannot recall why, but his nickname for me was 'Fingers'. I of course retaliated by christening him 'Fums' but it should really have been 'Knees' because he was very good at beating out the rhythm to a tune on that part of his anatomy with his hands. John left the Met Office before the Met Office left Dunstable, but we kept in touch over the years. He kept all the letters I ever wrote to him and kindly made this archive available to me. Reading things I had written so many years ago caused a little bit of embarrassment (did I really say that?), a little bit of puzzlement (who the hell was Norma?), but mostly an amazing and enjoyable re-awakening of memories that made parts of this book very much easier to write.

Tony Toombs joined my class at Dunstable Grammar after the thirteen plus exam and in a similar way joined the Met Office some time after me. I honestly can't remember what he did in the fairly brief meantime before coming into MO5A. If I was into motorbikes Tony was into cars – and what cars! Over the years he had a Morgan, a Jowett Jupiter and a Triumph TR2. It was Tony who first drove me over the magical 'ton' – 100mph and I think it was in a Triumph TR3 that he drove me to my wedding, but I do seem to remember him descending briefly to the depths of an ancient Ford 8 costing £15 at one stage of his motoring career. He parted company with the road a few times but fortunately never with me in the passenger seat. Tony eventually ended up working at the Road Research Laboratory near Bracknell and again we have kept in touch if only by exchanging Christmas Cards, but he was at my retirement party with his wife Jill.

Eric Hughes had unruly gingery hair and wore tortoiseshell-rimmed glasses with thick lenses. He was so laid-back that he was virtually horizontal and one of his favourite phrases was 'let's keep the situation fluid'. Eric's only transport was a bicycle with dropped handlebars that he called 'Maria' and he was a regular passenger in Tony's cars. He was in the 'dicky seat' one night (a young lady was occupying the front seat and probably also occupying the driver) when Tony made one of his excursions into a ditch. Tony clambered out, ascertained the he and his girl friend of the time were both OK but could find no sign of Eric in the car, in the ditch or anywhere on the verge. They were beginning to get desperate when the sound of gentle singing led them to look up and see Eric quite cheerfully spread-eagled in the tree to which he had been catapulted by the crash. Eric eventually transferred to another part of the civil service and was last heard of living in London in a 'residential hotel for gentlemen'.

1959 was a year of firsts and openings. The Morris Mini and Austin Mini 7 were launched in August and the M1 motorway was opened. Compared to today there was very little traffic on the motorway and of course no speed limit. It was a real pleasure to ride the Beezer on these wide-open spaces and smile at the very large numbers of cars on the hard shoulder that had overheated, had bits fall off or had just blown up because they weren't built for or used to sustained high speed. I had my first vote in a general election in October when the Conservatives under Harold MacMillan won. Not long before he had been telling us that 'we had never had it so good' and he was probably right. The Met Office opened its first Weather Centre in London and in January we saw the installation of our first computer Meteor built by Ferranti at a cost in excess of £100,000, which made my gross pay for 1958-59 of £322 look pretty small.

Meteor filled most of a large room but probably had far less memory and computing power than the fairly ancient PC that I am typing this on. It comprised yards of steel cabinets filled with electronics, with a desk and a control panel consisting of just a few toggle switches and two tiny circular cathode ray tubes that displayed binary blips as data was inputted and processed. The most prominent part of the control panel was the clock and this was very important, as computer time had to be booked by the various scientists and was jealously guarded. Input of programmes and data was all by punched paper tape produced by teleprinter, and output was either by paper tape or by the Bull Printer that was incredibly noisy and printed mechanically a whole row of text at a time on a continuous paper feed. The whole room was enclosed in a wooden frame covered in chicken wire to protect the computer

METEOR in action – an unidentified scientist is leaning against the Bull Printer and Joy Whitelam is at the controls. I just happened to be there when the photographer arrived and posed doing something totally unnecessary with the paper tape output

from outside electrical sources, and the computer itself had to be temperature controlled.

Most of our time now was spent extracting and processing data for use on the computer – basically turning pages of figures into yards of paper tape. It was about this time that I started working for Mr Freeman, who up until then had been something of a mystery figure, as he had spent every day literally locked into a tiny office dealing with weather observations connected with our hydrogen bomb tests at Christmas Island in 1957 which were still 'Top Secret'. Now that he had been let out of his cupboard he was developing a computer model that would hopefully predict visibility at Heathrow Airport. With amazing originality he christened his programme FOG and a later variant became FOB. He was very pleasant to work with and, because the job was very specific and the end result if it worked would obviously be very useful, it was an interesting project to be involved with.

Apart from cricket, tug of war and beer drinking in pubs, the long hot summer made impromptu parties at various flats and people's homes very popular, with very little excuse needed and with my usual crowd aided and abetted by characters like David 'Jim' Langley and by two former grammar schoolmates Pete Duffy and Jeff Bryson who had joined the office that year. I remember one party somewhere off West Street when, with bottle deposits at only a few old pennies, we went to the off-licence and got over £2 back in empties before 8pm. On another occasion we took a Walls Ice Cream sign from outside a shop during a raid from a party, kept it as a trophy and then arranged another party a week later to put it back in place at exactly the same time that it had been taken. Pete Duffy only stayed about a year and Jeff Bryson later

Barbara Steele splices together two lengths of the ubiquitous paper tape

joined the Metropolitan Police. 'Jim' Langley became joint editor of the sports and social club newsletter and I became a regular contributor, covering among other things the annual coach trip to the Farnborough Air Show in September. We also collaborated on the creation of a cartoon character called Nig Nog who made regular appearances in the sheet.

Also fitted into this summer was the usual family holiday in July when we rented a house called Tal-Llyn in Morfa Nefyn, North Wales. It can't have been over exciting as the highlights described in a letter to my mate John were going into Pwllheli by

Jeff Bryson, myself and Pete Ball
with the magically re-appearing ice cream sign

bus and playing Bobby Darin's Dream Lover five times on the juke box, but I also mentioned getting two dates with someone called Gwynneth of whom I have absolutely no memory. One memory that I think belongs to this holiday is that all the males stayed home one day while all the females went off shopping again to Pwllheli. Watching for them to return we were a bit surprised when the bus actually stopped right outside the house rather than at the proper stop. The reason became obvious as the conductor started to help Mum, Gran Maud and Aunty Gert unload a vast quantity of blankets and towels they had bought at the market – so many that they had bought a clothes line to rope them together! The look on Uncle Joe's face as this picture unfolded was amazing. Also amazing was the journey we undertook to get there. We probably had Ben Meachem's taxi to Luton and then by train to St Pancras. We then walked from St Pancras to Euston with all our suitcases to catch the 10.30pm, changing at Crewe and Bangor to arrive at Pwllheli at 7.24am. There we had breakfast in a café before taking the bus to Morfa Nefyn – overall journey time well over twelve hours!

On 26 October I was invited to attend a board and just over a month later I was told that I had been successful and my appointment was now 'permanent' with a pay rise to £360 a year. About a month again after that, I became 'established' and a real civil servant (but even the establishment was now subject to a further twelve months probation). Earlier in the year or even in 1958 I had applied to become an officer in the RAF and had attended a four-day selection course at RAF Hornchurch in Middlesex. If you failed any part of the process you were asked to pack your bag, so I was quite pleased still to be there at the end of the fourth

M.O.11 and M.O.12 Christmas lunch in the Dunstable canteen. Around the table are: Mike Holmes, myself, Liz Moore, ?, ?, David 'Jim' Langley, Joyce Hardes, ?, Pat Baker, Vena? and Sheila?

day. They offered me a ground commission but I had wanted to fly and decided to stay where I was. Now that I was permanent, though, I could apply for postings and there was one posting that would get me into the air as an Air Met Observer on the weather flight operating Shackletons out of RAF Aldergrove in Northern Ireland. I applied and promptly forgot all about it.

14

TO BOVINGDON AND BACK

In the previous chapter I mentioned the sport and the beer and the parties but didn't get round to talking about the girls. A minority of the parties were 'stag' affairs but most had an ample supply of members of the opposite sex. This was fine, but if there was any time left over after (in priority order) cricket, other sport, beer drinking, those parties and work, then every effort was made to fill at least some of that time by 'going out' with a girl. Many new entrants were sent to Dunstable, almost always to MO11 or MO12, for a few days or a few weeks before going off to training school and there was a fairly swift turnover of staff anyway, so there was a never-ending supply of opportunities. The motorbike could be an asset, as some of the girls would fancy a ride on the pillion even if they didn't fancy me quite as much. Once they were on the back there was a stretch of straight road that ran from the other side of Toddington (near when the M1 junction is now) to Fancott, where, if you hit the brow of the hill at the right speed, you could be airborne for a considerable distance. This could have quite a startling effect on some young ladies when you stopped at the little spinney just down the road (unless it had actually made them feel sick).

It was against this background that, towards the end of 1959, my mates bet me a night's free beer that I couldn't get a date with every new female entrant that came into Met Office, Dunstable. Having established that this wouldn't include a certain lady with a horrendous body odour problem who was already there, this was a challenge that couldn't possibly be resisted. In my quest I had two very good allies. Arthur 'Jock' Milton, our Admin man, was the first to receive advance notification of new arrivals and he was happy to provide me with this information to assist my planning. Invariably when new entrants arrived, they spent some time in the small reference library near the entrance to the research block that was run by a married lady called Yolande or Iolande Kyle. She was lovely, got me all sorts of background information on the prospective 'dates' and advised me on strategy. I called her my Aunty Yo and she became a special friend. The planning, the strategy and possibly my cheek paid off and I had a 100% success rate as February 1960 progressed. Some had been gorgeous, some had been complete dogs, some had been easy to persuade and some took a bit of persistence. I even managed a cinema date with one lady who was not only a good bit older than me but also Experimental Officer grade and that was almost unheard of. I received notification that I was being posted to RAF Bovingdon and it was decided that my move would be the cut-off date for the bet.

The move to Bovingdon was connected to my application for Air Met Observer duties for which I needed synoptic experience at an outstation, and I was quite looking forward to it. The station was only a few miles away in Hertfordshire and as I would be working shifts it would be fairly easy to keep in touch with my friends at Dunstable. Not long before I was due to go, Arthur Milton advised me that I would have one more challenge to deal with before I left. The challenge and the time I had to deal with it was shown in the 'comings and goings' section of the March newsletter which included:

Coupe H E Miss	A.Sc.	New Entrant	to	MO12	1.3.60
Jackson G W H	A.Sc.*	MO12	to	RAF Bovingdon	7.3.60

* They never could make their minds up whether we were Scientific Assistants or Assistants Scientific

The 1st was a Tuesday and the 7th a Monday – just four working days to meet the last challenge and to meet my future wife! Happily Haidee not only said yes to the date but also yes to a much more important question just over a year later. I'm not sure exactly when our date was, but my farewell 'do' was in the Eight Bells at lunchtime on the Friday, so that may give a clue. The same newsletter included a little farewell to me that concluded 'altogether a very fine contribution to the social life of the establishment during his first two years in the office'.

I had, or rather Mum and Maud had, arranged lodgings for me in Bovingdon with Mr and Mrs Dickens, who were cousins of some sort. They were friendly enough but it wasn't home, and all I remember clearly of my time there are the mashed potatoes being served with vast quantities of both butter and pepper. I soon decided that with the shift pattern I was working it would be easier to commute from home and easier to stay connected both to Haidee and that social life I had obviously been noted for in Dunstable. Haidee didn't go to training school until 9 May, so we had a reasonable amount of time to get to know each other better and for her to make a real impression on her first visit from training school to The Hyde by falling off her Vespa scooter on the gravel as she rode up to and almost into the front gate – quite an entrance. Haidee's Dad had bought the Vespa, PCE 852, for £92.15.4d taxed and insured, and it served her (and me at times) well for years to come.

In May I became involved in local politics for the very first time when Mum stood for election to the Parish Council and I helped by acting as a runner between the tellers at the various polling stations. Mum stood as one of eleven Independents calling themselves the Houghton Eleven but in actual fact they were all members of the Conservative Association. She got in and as far as I can ascertain was only the second ever woman to serve on the Council, which then had fifteen members. Three of the fifteen, Sidney Clarke, Tommy Strange and George Nye, were also elected to Luton Rural District Council.

I soon got into the routine of shift work, commuting on my BSA, and the operational work of an RAF station, although there was one memorable and never to be repeated occasion when I rode all the way to Bovingdon for an evening shift starting at 2pm only to find that I wasn't on until 10pm! The station was the joint home of an RAF Fighter Command Communications Squadron and a USAF Transport Squadron. The RAF operated some ancient Avro Ansons and De Havilland Devons, with the Ansons being apparently used exclusively for runs to the Channel Islands to collect duty free booze and tobacco for distribution around the whole of Fighter Command. One of the Anson pilots had flown fighter aircraft in WW2 and used to have everyone watching to see if this would be the day that he would cartwheel into the ground as he did 'split-arse turns' on every take-off when only a couple of feet off the ground. The CO had his own personal Gloster Meteor two-seater jet in which he did 'circuits and bumps' just to keep his flying hours up. Had I been there longer I could have put my name down for a back seat ride with him but this would have meant having to do parachute training first. The Americans operated Douglas DC3s DC4s and DC6s and the occasional Fairchild Packet and Flying Box Car to do who knows what.

There were enough of us Scientific Assistants to provide 24-hour cover; a forecaster who was officer in charge and I think there was a junior forecaster who assisted and took care of the shop when the main man was away. There was no night flying, so the forecasters basically worked days providing the RAF with local and route forecasts and the routes were never that long. There was a full crew on duty during the day but for most of the evening and all of the night you were on your own. There would be an RAF Flight Lieutenant and a couple of other ranks upstairs in the control tower, but they went to bed as soon as it got dark. Our two main tasks were hourly weather observations and plotting weather charts for use by the forecaster when he came in. For the weather obs we went outside at about five minutes to the hour to the little enclosure containing most of our instruments some distance from the control tower, and gazed knowledgeably at the sky before we read the instruments.

For each observation we would have to estimate total cloud cover (in eighths), amounts (in eighths), heights and classifications of all types of low, medium and high clouds and also estimate visibility. To help at night we had a searchlight that we could switch on shining straight up, to hit low cloud and work out the height

197

by calculating the angles. We would read from instruments wind speed and direction, atmospheric pressure, temperature, wet bulb temperature (to give dew point temperature after calculation) and note whether the barometer was rising, falling or steady. A note would also be made of current weather and weather during the past hour. This would all then have to be encoded into five figure groups and sent by teleprinter to our Group Station at Uxbridge; they would send all their groups observations to Dunstable and Dunstable would then re-broadcast everything to all UK stations and selected stations to the rest of the world. We also had to send a summary of the observation on a special form up to Air Traffic Control.

The first group of five figures would be your station identification, (Bovingdon was 669), next would be total cloud cover, wind speed and direction (Nddff) – for example 49015 would mean that there was 4/8 cloud and the wind was east at fifteen miles per hour. Next would be VVwwW – visibility, current weather and past weather. Three more groups of five figures would cover the rest of the observation followed by additional groups as required, all beginning with an 8 and relating to each type of cloud visible. When I say that Dunstable used to start sending out batches of observations on the printer sometimes sooner than five minutes past the hour, you can tell how quickly we had to observe, encode and type out. If it was an hour when our forecaster required a chart, we would then immediately start plotting from the data coming in on the printer direct on to a weather chart.

We had charts covering just the UK and a bit of Europe for hourly use, charts covering most of Europe and the Atlantic for use every three hours and even wider coverage for every six hours.

FORM 2309
(Revised 6/56)

M783194 BJ287 9/56 20m pads A.G.85. 655/3.

METEOROLOGICAL OFFICE AIR MINISTRY

WEATHER REPORT TO AIR TRAFFIC CONTROL

OFFICE Bovingdon   SERIAL No. 12

DATE 3.7.60.   TIME 1455 GMT.

AIRFIELD STATE — GREEN

1. QFY

QAN GEO 310 ° 09 knots (Surface Wind)

QBA yards OR 8 nautical miles (Visibility)

QNY NIL

(Present Weather)

QBB TRACE oktas (Cu) 3500 ft. (E *) (Cloud)

8 oktas (Sc) 5000 ft. (E *)

oktas ft. (*)

QNH 1016·4 mb. 30·02 in.

REMARKS

* Letter " E " is inserted when height is estimated.

2. ADDITIONAL INFORMATION

QFE 997·0 mb. 29·44 in. QNT knots (gusts)

QMU 64 (Air temp.) and 49 (Dew point) deg. C.

TIME OF ISSUE 1500 GMT.   _Gotthut_ Observer.

THIS RECEIPT TO BE RETURNED TO THE METEOROLOGICAL OFFICE.

DATE 3·7·60. TIME 1455 GMT. SERIAL No. 12

REPORT RECEIVED AT GMT.

BY

(Signature or initials) †

† When reports are telephoned the recipient is requested to repeat the message back and give the sender his name or initials for entry here on the Meteorological Office copy.

A typical hourly report sent 'upstairs' to Air Traffic Control

At stations like Bovingdon the forecaster would usually only require the midnight or 6am Altantic chart when he came in, a full UK chart every three hours and a part UK chart every hour. This requirement was reduced during the time I was at Bovingdon when we had a large machine installed that allowed Dunstable to send out 'radio facsimiles' of charts produced in the forecast room there, printing direct onto a large roll of special paper. Today you'd call it a Fax.

To plot an observation you would first have to locate the station's identification number, which was printed on the chart alongside a small circle. The circle was then used as the centre of the plot that consisted of both figures and symbols in both red and black ink. For speed we used ordinary wooden handled dip pens, shortened, shaped to suit your grip and taped together so that they could be simultaneously dipped into red and black inkwells and switched from colour to colour as you worked. For example in just one group of figures visibility (VV) was in red, current weather (ww) in black and past weather (W) in red again. Temperature (TT) was in black and Dew Point Temperature (TdTd) was in red. Low and Medium cloud symbols (Cl and Cm) were in black and High cloud symbols (Ch) were in red. Add to these complications and the need for speed the fact that with many stations close together plots had to be very small but still totally readable and the fact that the forecaster was invariably at you shoulder waiting to get his hands and pencil on the chart, and you can imagine that during the day at least it was not the doddle I had been used to in MO12.

The prescribed lay-out for a 'plot' on a standard weather chart. Each plot had to be small enough to fit under a pre-decimal sixpence

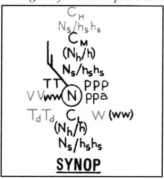

Code figure	N	W	C_L	C_M	C_H	C	a
0							
1							
2							
3							
4							
5							
6							
7							
8							
9							

Symbols for cloud cover (N), weather in the past hour (W), cloud types (CL CM CH and C) and pressure movement (a)

ww	0	1	2	3	4	5	6	7	8	9
0										
1										
2										
3										
4										
5										
6										
7										
8										
9										

Symbols for current weather (ww) – for example 83 = sleet showers

It was when I was en-route to Bovingdon for a night duty that I had my worst accident on the motorbike. I was riding along a main road minding my own business on a warm summer evening. It was still light and you could see for miles, but an idiot female in a Morris Minor with 'L' plates decided to pull out in front of me. I swerved to pass behind the car but instead of carrying on she panicked and stopped dead. I still almost made it round behind but just made contact with the over-rider on her back bumper. By now I was in the side road and had no way back to the main road except through a garage forecourt, which I made with a bit if jiggling and a bit of kerb mounting to actually pass between two petrol pumps before regaining the road. I stopped the bike and jumped off to go back and give the female a severe talking to, took one step and fell in a heap. It was then that I discovered that it hadn't been the bike that had hit the car, it had been my ankle.

The injury didn't seem too bad, so I got back on the bike and rode the few miles further to RAF Bovingdon where I got off and found my shoe full of blood. With the help of the evening man I patched it up and hobbled through the shift, but by the time the morning man came on I was really suffering. He kick-started the bike for me and helped me mount up and I made it home. Luckily nothing was broken and I had a few days off to let it scab over and for the swelling to go down. It was my worst motorcycle injury and I never parted company with the bike. Strangely enough, a couple of years later exactly the same could be said of Haidee and it was the same foot!

Night shifts were really boring; after you had finished plotting the midnight chart there was virtually nothing to do other than the hourly observations for almost four hours. We had a radio but the BBC closed all its stations down at or before midnight. Radio Luxembourg and Radio Hilversum in Holland carried on a bit longer but by about 1am there was nothing to do except read, write and doodle. The same was true of Sundays when there was usually no flying. I did a lot of reading – still into the Pan paperbacks - a lot of writing, including letters to John Hall and to Haidee while she was away, and a number of articles for the Dunstable newsletter despite the fact that I was no longer there.

Bovingdon had its own newsletter called for some unfathomable reason Duck Billed Platypus and I re-jigged a couple of old Dunstable newsletter articles for it and also did some new bits and pieces including some rather Goon-like mock adverts such as:

> Are you tired, listless, slow on the job, unable to talk to even casual acquaintances? Then stop being a switchboard operator NOW.

and

> Are you lonely? Do people cross the road to avoid you? They do?
> Try going for walks without your tiger.

and little questions such as:

> If the wind is gusting at 25 knots and then slackens off – is this
> Dis-gusting?

Despite being at Bovingdon my social life stayed firmly anchored around Dunstable. Tony Toombs had sold his Morgan and bought a Jowett Jupiter that was immediately christened Red Death. Jowett was a very small company that made Bradford vans with both three and four wheels, a strange flat backed saloon called the Javelin and the sports car Jupiter that was rarer than hen's teeth. In one evening out with Tony I visited the Crown at Houghton Regis, the Spread Eagle, the Nag's Head, the Red Lion, the White Horse and the Eight Bells, partaking along the way quantities of Manns KK, Benskins Best and Flowers Kegmaster and finishing with a whisky and pep! No problems with such things as breathalysers in those days! I was almost certainly wearing my new Robin Hood hat with natty feathers that had been popularised by the comedian Tony Hancock and was all the rage at the time.

Then there was the mushrooming – 1960 must have been a good year for them as I regularly filled the pannier boxes on the bike. Usually there were plenty for everyone, but on a couple of occasions I had cleared the field before the RAF got up and I was able to name my price in cigarettes for barter from panic stricken lower ranks unable to find enough mushrooms for the Flight Lieutenant's breakfast. I had always loved mushrooms, particularly fried with bacon, and as a very young lad I remember on more than one occasion being woken up in what was the middle of the night for me and coming down to the kitchen to share in a mushroom feast. These were mushrooms brought as a treat by a family friend Jim Kefford who had picked them at his then workplace – RAF Bovingdon. So it really was a case of back to my childhood when I came home from the very same airfield with my own supply for breakfast. But despite this bounty of nature and despite quite enjoying the work at Bovingdon, before the end of the summer I had decided that I would forget Air Met Observing and go back to the mates I had never really left and to my now 'steady' girlfriend Haidee. On 19 August, less than six months after leaving, I applied for a posting back to Dunstable. One final memory of Bovingdon is a conversation with SAC Smith who was one of the cheerier members of Air Traffic Control and made regular visits to our office for a chat. He was talking about his girl friend and said 'last night I finally got her to say yes.' 'Congratulations.' I said, 'when's the wedding?' 'Wedding?' says SAC Smith, 'what wedding?

My posting didn't take too long to come through and I was very soon learning yet another new job 'on the bench' in MO5(A). Basically our job was to receive and distribute weather observations from and to all over the world. The heart of the department was the Editing Room and this was strategically placed between the communications section with its banks of teleprinters and radioteleprinters and the Forecast Room. We were all connected by a system of moving belts and chutes. As the broadcasts of hourly observations came in on the teleprinters from UK group stations and from collection centres all over the world, they would be ripped off the print roll during pauses in transmission in lengths ranging from a few inches to a few feet and be sent along the conveyors to us. They would usually be three ply with thin carbons between but the new NCR (no carbon required) paper was just coming into use. Everything would arrive first with the senior person on the shift, who was given a posh name I can't remember but something like 'collator'. He or she would remove any garbled or blank sections by use of a ruler and a quick tear, pass one copy through to the Forecast Room for plotting on charts and distribute the other copies down chutes to the 'Editor' or 'Bench Editors', with all the rubbish and carbon papers going into a huge bin. We would then mark up and send back down the conveyor observations for re-broadcast to various places and also extract certain observations for particular uses. It was a lot more complicated than this but I won't bore you with detail. One particular job for example was to decode a small number of station observations, turn them into English and phone them through to the BBC – these followed the shipping forecast as 'weather reports from coastal stations' and would read something like 'Stornaway: Wind West Northwest Force Seven, persistent rain, 996 millibars, falling slowly'.

I was now very much part of Dunstable's operational heart that comprised the Forecast Room, which was responsible for all national and international forecasts, the Editing Room, which sorted and distributed weather data, the Communications Room, which received and sent everything the other two dealt with, and last but not least, CRDF (Cathode Ray Direction Finding), which used fairly basic Radar at various locations in the UK to locate thunderstorms with all the reports being coordinated at Dunstable. One of the stalwarts of CRDF was a man called Lofty Spain whose name became part of a catchphrase after one of our female colleagues totally unconsciously threw into a conversation the classic line 'Lofty Spain was thunderstruck'!

By the nature of the job, it was very hectic for about twenty-five minutes in every hour and fairly peaceful for the rest. This enabled us on night duty, once the midnight rush was over, to take it in turns to double up and do two jobs and get a couple of hours sleep in the rest room. For the rest of the time, particularly in the evenings when the bosses who worked days had gone home, the Devil found work for idle hands and in cooperation with my old mate Tony Toombs I started up my first underground newspaper, the Bench

Express. This was produced on one of the special typewriters that were built to take one of the three-ply teleprinter rolls, so we always had three copies of every edition. There were usually four or five pages of spoof adverts and tongue in cheek news items gently taking the micky out of our bosses, our workmates and ourselves. We also produced in 1961 a single sheet Official List of Recommended Hostelries and Places of Interest in Dunstable and its Environs. This included:

> **The Eight Bells:**
> A modern ideally situated public house one minute from the Editing Room. Pleasant music can be heard as a background at most times. Watney-Mann's Ales can be obtained.

> **The Union Cinema:**
> A rather small but nevertheless comfortable cinema belonging to the ABC circuit. Continuous programmes from 1.15pm approx.

> **The California Ballroom:**
> A place of interest to all who are young at heart. Music pleases the ear and liquor flows from 8 – 11.45pm thrice weekly. Many famous pop stars appear and there is also a lido and roller skating rink.

> **The Meteorological Office:**
> A place of little interest to thinking people. It was thrown together during World War 2 and has since been forgotten by the general public.

Mention of the 'Cali' brings back some memories. On hot summer days groups of us would often go for a swim in the pool after work or even during our lunch break. The acts were often quite good in the ballroom and I particularly recall the Allisons at the time of their (only) Top Ten hit, Are you Sure, and Kathy Kirby. Kathy Kirby was particularly memorable for her lip gloss and for the fact that at the California there was a gallery bar from where you could lean over a rail and look down on the stage and on this occasion straight down the front of Kathy's dress!

On Saturday November 5 1960, The Hyde became the venue for a major social event, the invitation for which read as follows:

Programme	
7.30pm	Bonfire to be lit.
7.30pm – 8.30pm	General bonfire festivities, etc.
8.30pm	Light refreshments and alcoholic beverages to be served in the house.
9.00pm onwards	Swing to the music of 'Fingers' Jackson and his three-speed record player featuring John 'Ted' Hall on the knees and Eric 'Larwood' Hughes on the floor.

Drinks available throughout the evening. Seats provided, beds extra. Please bring along a few fireworks and some bottles (preferably full).

A great time was had by all, especially by Eric Hughes and by my brother Nigel who had decided to assume the role of Eric's personal glass-filler. Eric's glass was never empty despite his very best efforts and Nigel, aged 9, was well away on an occasional sip and the fumes!

15

GOODBYE HOUGHTON

As 1960 drew to an end there was increasing speculation and uncertainty about the impending closure of Met Office, Dunstable, and the transfer of all operations to new purpose-built premises in Bracknell, Berkshire. There were briefings and reports on the design and build of the new office block that were not always reassuring. One report said that some pillars could be removed from the Forecast Room as 'they merely supported the roof'. We were also told that we need have no fear of fire as 'the building will not burn, only the things in it'. As one of the guys at the meeting said 'well, speaking as one of the things in it!' Whether it was this uncertainty or whether we were all a bit fed up, a number of us applied for jobs elsewhere.

On 2nd December, I had an interview with Burroughs, who made adding machines, had premises in Luton Road, Dunstable and were moving into computers. I honestly can't remember whether they turned me down or I turned them down, but I think that I decided to stay where I was, at least for the time being. If that was the way of it, it was a good decision because the company's venture into computers was short-lived and fairly disastrous. The following day John Hall had a job offer from J Lyons & Co, who were better known for making ice cream and running Corner

House restaurants but who were now going into computing in a big way with their LEO computer. John was by now 'going steady' with Janet Walton, a local girl my family knew, as her father worked for one of the undertakers that Gran Maud 'laid out' for. It was probably after a lot of thought therefore that he decided to take the job, which was in London.

John's last day at the Met Office was on 27th January 1961 and the occasion was marked in the usual way at the Eight Bells. For some reason lost in the mists of time, I presented John with a liquid soap container that, believe it or not, he still has. The following day, John came with Haidee and me to what is probably the most memorable football match I have ever attended. It was an FA cup match at Kenilworth Road where Luton were playing Manchester City in mist and torrential rain. We saw Dennis Law score six excellent goals and Luton were losing 6 – 2 when the referee suddenly decided to abandon the match because of fog or the state of the pitch, no-one was really sure. Amazingly, Luton won the rearranged game 3 – 1 and again Dennis Law was City's only scorer. John travelled up to his new home in Ealing and started work with LEO on the Monday.

In February, another era came to an end with the death of Colonel Part of Houghton Hall, and Gran Maud received a very nice hand written response from Lady Part to her letter of condolence. With Haidee, I made good use of the double seats in the back row of the cinema in Biggleswade and we went to a dance in a village hall – in Guilden Morden, I think, where we saw a rock and roll band from Bedford called The Kingpins who were very good, better than many who had recording contracts at that time. Spring was obviously in the air as I had popped the question, Haidee had said yes and we had decided we would like to get engaged.

We chose a diamond and emerald ring that cost 15 guineas – almost exactly two week's pay before tax, and on Sunday 19 March I rode my BSA to Midfields at Wrestlingworth for Sunday lunch and to do things properly by asking Douglas Coupe for his only daughter's hand in marriage. The fields around were snowy but the reception was far from frosty and he said he was sure I would look after her well. Both Douglas and his wife June almost certainly thought we were far too young to be thinking of marriage, but with us both soon moving to Bracknell I suppose it made some sort of sense to them and both sets of parents were totally supportive. Mum was quite friendly with a Dunstable Gazette reporter who wrote under the name of 'Pearl', so the next time we were at The Hyde she appeared complete with photographer and we made quite a spread in the next edition.

A few days later my feet were firmly back on the ground with the cricket AGM where I took over from John Hall as Secretary. In the report on the 1960 season I was able to tell the meeting that we had won 13 of the 23 matches we had played and had been much more successful in the shorter evening games where we had won 10 and lost only to RAF Stanbridge. Ken Saunders, Mike Collins and Eric Hughes had been our most successful bowlers, with Eric bowling 55 overs more than any other bowler and bowling 22 overs at only 2.5 runs per over in the game against the Empire Rubber Company. The skipper, Bernard Evans, had been our best batsman and we had lost just one game to the weather in the whole summer. A little later in the year I was able to report to John Hall on matches we had played against Chalney Schoolmasters, the Ariel Club, Bagshawe's and RAF Halton and an amazing 7 wicket

The engagement photograph. [photo: Courtesy Dunstable Gazette]

win against Index Printers when Tony Toombs took a remarkable 5 wickets for 5 runs. I seem to recall sinking several celebratory beers that night.

On 12 April 1961, I was on duty in the Editing Room when a piece of teleprinter roll came down the conveyor belt. It was from Moscow, in plain language rather than the usual five figure code groups, and read as follows:

'SOVIET CITIZEN, COMMUNIST YURI GAGARIN, PIONEER OF SPACE EXPLORATION. YURI GARGARIN THANKED THE HEAD OF THE SOVIET GOVERNMENT FOR HIS TELEGRAM OF GREETINGS.

I AM HAPPY TO REPORT TO YOU, THE COSMONAUT SAID, THAT THE FIRST SPACE FLIGHT HAS BEEN SUCCESSFULLY COMPLETED.

KRUSCHEV AGAIN CONGRATULATED YURI GARGARIN. BY YOUR FEAT, HE SAID, YOU HAVE GLORIFIED OUR COUNTRY, DISPLAYED COURAGE AND HEROISM IN THE FULFILMENT OF THIS RESPONSIBLE MISSION.

BY YOUR EXPLOIT YOU HAVE MADE YOURSELF IMMORTAL, BECAUSE YOU ARE THE FIRST MAN TO HAVE BEEN IN OUTER SPACE'

There was a lot more in the same vein. It was amazing to us – dogs and monkeys had been sent up but no-one expected a manned space flight, nor for the Russians to beat the Americans, and I was among the first to know as the teleprinter message, which I still have, came in well before the news came out on British radio and TV. It was 5th May before the yanks caught up and put Alan Shepherd into space.

Three more things of note happened before the move to Bracknell. In April a party from the office went on an evening guided tour of AC-Delco. It was a real eye-opener for us because, as I said in a newsletter article covering the trip, 'many of us had seen work being done for the first time'. If nothing else it convinced me I had made the right choice in not becoming an apprentice there. On May 16th John and Janet announced their engagement and joined a growing club of Met Office and ex-Met Office staff getting married or engaged. In June, we went to the Rootes Motors Field Day and saw my sister Jennifer crowned Miss Commer. I thought at the time that I must have been getting old if my little sister was old enough to be a beauty queen!

The move to Bracknell was staggered over a fairly long period and the two research departments MO11 and MO12 were among the first to go. Haidee moved in the summer, July I think, and was found a bed-sitter near Ascot. I made the trip down as often as possible which was sometimes made difficult by the irregular shift pattern I was then working, with eight or nine days on followed by two or three days off. Days were 9am-5pm, Mornings were 8am-2pm, Evenings were 2pm-10pm and Nights were 10pm-8am and a typical run at this time would have been: D M M E E M M/N N - - - E, etc., with the first Night normally being on the same day

Jennifer becomes Miss Commer 1961. [photo: Courtesy Dunstable Gazette]

as the last Morning. I was scheduled to move on 29 September and the one memorable event during this intervening period was the first strike of civil servants for some very considerable time. It was just a one-day stoppage in an attempt to secure better pay and conditions and was even supported by the ultra moderate Institute of Professional Civil Servants, which was my 'union'. I duly took the day off to go down to Bracknell to see Haidee and was punished by having to spend most of the day getting a replacement chain for my motorbike after the original had spectacularly disintegrated en-route.

The move to Bracknell eventually happened and the transfer of operations went very smoothly considering that twenty-four hour services had to be maintained throughout. I became a resident at Holly Springs, Jiggs Lane, Bracknell, which was an old mansion that the Met Office had converted for use as a hostel. In a letter to John Hall, I described it as follows:

'There are bedrooms sleeping 2, 3, 4 and 5. Each person has a bed, a dressing table, a wardrobe, a chair and a bedside table. Sheets, blankets and towels are provided and laundered free. We have a large kitchen with every pot and pan imaginable provided and we can cook what we like when we like. We also have a laundry complete with washing machine, spin drier, irons and ironing boards. We also have a lounge with settees and armchairs. Papers are delivered daily and we have a TV as well. There are no restrictions on time to get in and we can have any visitors we like (not in bedrooms though). I am in a four-bed room with Tony, Eric and Bill Pendleton. The cost is 26 shillings a week plus four shillings and sixpence a month for the TV and papers. Haidee is quite happily installed in her bed-sitter and I am allowed to visit her three nights a week.'

Those restrictions on visits seemed quite natural at the time!

I think Tony and I were a day or so ahead of Eric and Bill Pendleton in moving in and we chose a large airy bedroom at the head of the very imposing staircase and quite close to the communal toilets and bathrooms (there were washbasins in the rooms). The room we thought was the best in the house and I decided that it should have something to indicate its superior status and naturally the superior status of its occupants. I noticed that in the lounge there was a huge mirror with a heavy carved frame over the fireplace and at the top of this frame was a beautifully carved coat of arms about twelve inches high. Closer examination showed that it was held in place by just two screws and that the frame actually looked better without it. Those same two screws soon had it fixed firmly to the outside of our bedroom door and it became such a permanent fixture that when decorators came in to do some tidying up a few weeks later they actually removed the coat of arms, varnished the door, put the carving back and varnished that as well. It was still there when I left.

Following the move, I was fairly affluent for a time, as I got a transfer grant of £20 and a subsistence allowance of £45 covering the move period. I would also be getting back pay of more than £68 as, possibly due to the strike, I would receive a fairly massive 12% pay-rise backdated in part for two years on 1 January and on my 21st birthday in May 1962 my gross pay would go up to £500 a year, halfway to what we considered to be the magic 'rich people's' £1,000. The new offices and operational rooms were a great improvement on what we had been used to at Dunstable but were much less conducive to socialising, being full of people we didn't know from London, Harrow, Stanmore and other establishments that had now all come under the same roof, having the former Dunstable departments spread throughout what was a large building, having few communal facilities and most of all not having a field! John Hall came to visit in November and I made a note at that time that Tony Toombs was 'still roaring around in red death'.

So began my life away from Houghton Regis. I married Haidee in 1962 and we returned as fairly frequent visitors until Mum and Dad finally moved away in the 1970s, but even as I left for Berkshire the village was fast changing and was on the path to becoming somewhere I no longer quite felt part of, somewhere I would no longer really want to be and somewhere almost unrecognisable as the Houghton of my youth. But the older I become, the more I realise that the Houghton Regis of my youth is very much part of me and part of what I am today.

APPENDIX 1

DECEASED LAID OUT BY MAUD HUMPHREY

The list below is taken from my grandmother's own handwritten records. In 1956 when she retired from AC-Delco she started a new book and transcribed earlier records into it. Some may have been lost in this process but it is thought that the entries are virtually complete. The lack of entries during the 1940s and early 1950s is due to her being in full time employment at that time.

DATE	NAME	AGE	U/TAKER	CHARGE £ s d
09.11.22	Jane Hickingbottom	59	Webb	0.11.0
01.23	Jeffery Gadsden	73	Webb	0. 8.6
17.02.24	Harry Turvey	77	Webb	0. 8.0
06.24	Phoebe Messenger	79	Webb	0.11.0
25.11.24	Charles Kempson	43	Franklin	0. 5.0
28.12.24	William Groom	81	Franklin	0. 9.9
01.01.25	Ann Groom	77	Franklin	0.11.0
07.02.25	Ann Bird	59	Webb	0.11.0
12.03.25	Jane Humphrey	75	Webb	0. 9.0
18.04.25	William Anstee	84	Webb	0.12.0
28.08.25	George Tompkins	84	Webb	0.16.3
11.09.25	Mary Ann Hazel	72	Webb	0.10.6
15.10.25	Joseph Clark	53	Webb	0.10.6

23.01.26	Emily Bowler	62	Webb	0.12.6
unknown	Ann Sinfield	72	Webb	0. 8.0
unknown	Gertrude Hathaway	56	Franklin	0.12.6
unknown	Albert Charles Kingham	59		0. 7.6
unknown	Jane Harris	75	Webb	0.10.0
15.06.29	John Horsler	94	Ashwell	0.12.6
29	Mary Jane Goosey	83	Webb	0.15.0
18.06.29	George Tompkins	83	Webb	0.16.0
21.06.29	Mary Ann Turvey	80	Webb	0. 5.6
04.07.29	Annie Smith	49	Franklin	0.17.6
17.08.29	George Jefford	76	Webb	0.15.0
07.11.29	Lavinia O C Bartholomew	58	Franklin	0.15.0
20.01.30	Elizabeth Willis	73	Webb	0.10.0
03.30	Reginald A D Foster	9 m	Franklin	0. 2.6
09.05.30	John Fensome	83	Franklin	0.16.6
11.07.30	George Henry Fowler	68	Webb	0.15.0
27.08.30	Joseph Ballard	67	Franklin	0.15.0
09.10.30	Alfred William Dumpleton	16	Webb	0.10.6
16.01.31	Charles Impey	86	Franklin	0. 1.0
07.05.31	Edith Martha Cook	52	Ashwell	0.15.0
14.10.31	Louisa Emma Foster	60	Franklin	0.15.0
12.11.31	Fanny Kelly	73	Franklin	0.17.0
02.12.31	Rosina Mary Long	65	Franklin	0.16.0
31.12.31	William Evans	81	Webb	0.12.6
18.03.32	Alice Elizabeth Beckwith (cousin)	44	Franklin	0. 5.0
18.12.32	Eva May Dumpleton	21	Webb	0.10.9
31.12.32	Alfred Smith	77	Webb	0.13.3
02.02.33	Richard Sharp	71	Webb	0.17.0

02.03.33	George Pedder	62	Webb	0.15.0
10.33	Thomas William Parker	67	Franklin	0.17.6
19.07.33	Lucy Lily Blow		Ashwell	1. 5.0
26.04.34	Mildred Ann Massey Thompson	68	Webb	0.19.6
03.06.34	Jane East	73	Webb	0.11.0
01.10.34	Elizabeth Dickens	71	Franklin	0.15.6
20.10.34	William Dyke	71	Webb	0.11.0
09.03.35	Herbert Bird	67	Webb	0.14.0
03.04.35	Edith Williams Mellor	67	Neville	0.10.0
23.04.35	Bertha Copperwaite	62	Franklin	0.17.6
04.03.36	Ellen Hedges	89	Franklin	1. 1.0
29.04.36	Hannah Harris	66	Neville	1. 0.0
26.04.36	Lenora Saunders	85	Neville	0.13.9
09.06.36	Elizabeth Cooper	66	Neville	0.17.0
12.06.36	Elizabeth Bright	85	Neville	0.15.0
20.07.36	Charlotte Castle	66	Franklin	1. 5.0
13.02.37	Thomas Bird	69	Ashwell	0.17.6
28.04.37	George Collier	71	Franklin	0.13.6
37	George Homewood	82	Franklin	1. 6.0
14.01.38	Elizabeth East	72	Franklin	0.13.6
27.01.39	Joseph George Scroggs	71	Neville	0.15.6
39	William Edward Ryle	71	Neville	1. 3.6
08.39	Joseph Tomlinson	74	Franklin	1. 0.0
21.09.39	Ann Elizabeth Burnage			nil
39	Rosie Mary Troon		Franklin	1. 3.6
41	Augustus Edward Chappell	61		nil
03.07.52	Gertrude Elizabeth Cockersole	72	Franklin	nil
21.11.52	Keith Robert Hamilton	4	Franklin	nil
07.06.56	Thomas Lawlor	71	Bates	1.10.0

221

01.07.56	George William Mead	83	Bates	3. 0.0
08.02.57	George William Loft	76	Neville	3. 0.0
16.08.57	Lily Bright Cemetery Road	63	Bates	2. 0.0
15.10.57	Emily Violet Clarke High Street	77	Bates	3.10.0
15.10.57	Thomas Reynolds Bishop King Street	76	Ashwell	3.10.0
25.10.57	Louisa Marsh High Street	93	Ashwell	3.10.0
15.12.57	Florence Bird Park Avenue	81	Bates	3.10.0
15.12.57	Harold Bright Sundon Road	64	Smith	2.10.0
20.01.58	Kate Bunker Chalk Hill	82	Bates	3. 0.0
04.03.58	Mary Elizabeth Smith Workhouse Row	88	Bates	2. 0.0
23.03.58	Florence Elizabeth Kingham Bidwell		Neville	2.15.0
24.03.58	Ellen Louisa Dickens	74	Bates	1.18.0
17.04.58	Arthur William Bunker Chalk Hill	84	Bates	3. 0.0
09.05.58	Florence Alice Hilpress	79	Bates	2.10.0
25.07.58	Lizzie Rawlings	83	Neville	3. 0.0
26.09.58	Bertha Mary Toseley	78	Bates	2. 5.0
05.10.58	Mary Jane Badstevener	83	Co-op	1.10.0
29.12.58	Gladys Minnie M G Tompkins	51	Bates	3. 0.0
05.04.59	Gladys May Gosbell	57	Bates	2.10.0
31.12.59	Thomas Henry Townsend	78	Bates	0.10.0
11.01.60	Mabel Mary Davis	76	Ashwell	7. 0.0
11.03.60	Fred Dumpleton	74	Smith	0.10.0
09.04.60	George William Brookfield Kurz	61	Co-op	2.10.0

18.04.60	Arthur Bright	65	Bates	3. 0.0
28.08.60	Arthur Smith	76	Bates	2.10.0
25.09.60	Thomas Peach	74	Bates	3. 0.0
30.09.60	Harry Perry	69	Bates	2.10.0
12.10.60	Albert William Oxenford	70	Bates	2.10.0
31.10.60	Cissie Oakley	70	Ashwell	3.10.0
15.11.60	Herbert Chandler	79	Bates	2.10.0
09.01.61	Lucy Gower	88	Bates	2.10.0
10.02.61	Jessie Elizabeth Parker	76	Bates	2.10.0
30.03.61	Nora Mary Smith	62	Neville	2. 0.0
01.04.61	Daniel McGilligan Leafields	71	Bates	3. 0.0
12.04.61	Ronald Clifford Sinfield	53	Bates	2.10.0
16.04.61	Frederick Dyer Graham Road	75	Bates	3.10.0
23.04.61	George Frederick Hyde	73	Bates	2. 4.0
04.06.61	Rose Annie Townsend	80	Bates	1. 0.0
16.06.61	Walter Reuben Gates Sundon Road	94	Neville	2. 0.0
26.09.61	Amy Startup Townsend Terrace	58	Bates	3.10.0
23.11.61	Clara Emily Wilds Poynters Road	85	Bates	3. 0.0
07.12.61	Reginald Arthur Dorrington St Michaels Avenue	64	Bates	3. 0.0
19.01.62	Richard Wrigglesworth Park Avenue	93	Bates	3. 0.
08.03.62	Nina Elizabeth Georgina Baker Woodlands Avenue	72	Bates	3. 0.0
26.04.62	Ellen Denton East Hill Lane	81	Neville	2. 0.0
19.05.62	Louisa Florence Elizabeth Fitzgerald		Bates	3. 0.0

24.05.62	Alice Skelton	71	Bates	3. 0.0
23.06.62	George Henry Purton Queen Street	71	Bates	3. 0.0
11.07.62	Sarah Lilian Russell	67	Bates	3. 7.0
13.07.62	May Dunderdale Houghton Road	80	Bates	3. 0.0
18.07.62	Leonard Hoskin Edward Street	67	Bates	3.10.0
20.07.62	Amelia Lloyd	65	Bates	3. 0.0
28.07.62	**Gertrude Germaine (sister)**	**63**	**Bates**	**nil**
03.09.62	Lizzie Bird Manor Park	67	Bates	4. 0.0
30.09.62	Emily Elizabeth Dixon Croft Green	88	Bates	3. 0.0
14.11.62	Alice Queenie Lovell Brookfields	68	Bates	3.10.0
05.11.62	Archibald Fensome	47	Neville	2.10.0
27.12.62	Nellie Webb Pond Bank	87	Neville	2.10.0
28.12.62	Clara Edith Bright Hillborough Road (Wembley)	65	Bates	0.10.0
31.01.63	Albert Charles Allen	69	Bates	3. 0.0
03.02.63	Alfred Edwin Wraight Mill Road	71	Co-op	2.10.0
07.05.63	Annie Hortensia Randall Park Avenue	85	Neville	2.10.0
22.05.63	Caroline Annie Giltrow Drury Lane	60	Co-op	2.12.0
13.06.63	Sidney James Handroff	58	Bates	4. 0.0
14.06.63	Beatrice Gosbell Bedford Road	80	Bates	3. 0.0
21.06.63	Joan Venn Woodlands Avenue	44	Bates	4. 0.0

09.07.63	Emma Allen Red House, The Green	87	Neville	2. 0.0
04.08.63	Arthur Ernest Roblett Tavistock Place	59	Bates	3. 0.0
10.09.63	Edgar Albert Avery Cumberland Street	77	Bates	3.15.0
14.10.63	Martha Isabella Burton Brookfields	47	Bates	3.10.0
22.10.63	Alfred Patrick Crawley Woodlands Avenue	69	Bates	3. 0.0
13.12.63	Thomas Francis Pratt East Hill Lane	74	Bates	3. 0.0
16.12.63	Caroline Elizabeth Kilbourne Woodlands Avenue	48	Smith	3.14.0
19.12.63	Dan Bird Manor Park	80	Bates	3. 0.0
27.01.64	Nellie Clara Tansley Fish Shop, High Street	66	Co-op	2.10.0
16.02.64	Edith Watson Malmsey Road	79	Co-op	2.12.0
08.03.64	Robert Lawson Eccles Hillborough Crescent	73	Bates	3. 5.0
14.03.64	Walter Edgar Fry Poynters Ro	77	Bates	3.10.0
05.04.64	Alice Edith Hill Leafields	77	Neville	2.10.0
16.04.64	Percy William Thomas Townsend Terrace	64	Bates	2.10.0
19.04.64	Louisa Wellford Malmsey	80	Bates	3. 0.0
25.04.64	Millicent Smith (cousin)	71		free
07.07.64	Karol Lukasiewicz West Parade	65	Bates	3. 0.0
10.07.64	William Bird Chiltern Road	61	Bates	3. 7.6

02.11.64	John Sandford Cumberland Street	81	Bates	3. 0.0
07.01.65	Frank Bird The Green	86	Bates	3. 0.0
19.02.65	Stanley Jack Field Park Avenue	51	Bates	4. 0.0
23.02.65	Olive Beryl Lovegrove Cumberland Street	64	Bates	4. 0.0
01.03.65	Arthur Gower Cumberland Street	71	Bates	3.10.0
27.03.65	Mabel Peel 14 Ridgeway Road, Dunstable	78	Bates	4. 0.0
08.04.65	Clifton William Thomas Kensworth	71	Bates	3. 0.0
14.04.65	Jean Robertson Quelch	28		1. 5.0
29.04.65	Thomas Edward Kiel Malmsey Road	82	Bates	3. 5.0
08.05.65	Elsie Margaret Davies King Street	66	Bates	3.10.0
06.06.65	Ernest Sydney Saunders Luton Road, Dunstable	68	Bates	3. 0.0
06.06.65	Cyril Cook Capron Road	74	Bates	3.10.0
06.08.65	Flora Hurst King Street	95	Bates	1. 0.0
27.08.65	Frederick George Bonham West Street	87	Bates	3. 0.0
10.10.65	Maud Elizabeth Mead Douglas Crescent	57	Bates	4. 0.0
20.11.65	William Brown Ridgeway Road	85	Bates	4. 0.0
11.12.65	Elsie Florence Paul Tithe Farm Road	76	Bates	3. 0.0
22.12.65	Florence Turner Bidwell Hill	73	Smith	2.16.0

09.01.66	Sidney Fred Bright Park Avenue	79	Neville	4. 0.0
26.01.66	Ada Mortlock 1 Grove Road	85	Co-op	0. 5.0
66	Ada Victoria Austin	68	Bates	4. 0.
11.03.66	Sylvia Clarke Brookfields	44	Bates	3. 0.0
02.04.66	Mary Ann Webb	78	Bates	3.10.0
23.04.66	Richard Arthur Davis Leafields	84	Bates	3.10.0
08.05.66	Charles Thomas Hallford Catherine Drive	73	Bates	3.10.0
26.05.66	Robert McWhirter Hybanks, The Green	71	Bates	3. 0.0
05.06.66	Martha Ellen Alston 128 High Street North, Dunstable	92	Bates	3.10.0
05.08.66	Charles Cheshire 24 Manor Park	88	Bates	3. 0.0
01.09.66	Beatrice May Hough 3 Vicarage Road	73	Bates	3. 0.0
31.10.66	Ada Florence Hooper 139 Tithe Farm Road	69	Bates	3. 0.0
10.12.66	Charles William Catling 17 Bidwell Hill	58	Bates	3. 0.0
28.01.67	Arthur Edward Kilbourne Woodlands Avenue	56	Bates	3. 0.0
05.03.67	Guy Scott Pigden 7 Harvey Road, Dunstable	6	Bates	3. 0.0
08.03.67	**Rose Thomson** **34 Winfield Street, Dunstable** **(sister)**	**69**	**Bates**	**free**
22.05.67	Edith Mabel Phillips 6 Cherry Tree Walk	78	Bates	3. 0.0
02.06.67	William Henry Adams Ferndale, Cumberland Street	77	Bates	3. 0.0

30.06.67	Albert Edward Peel 14 Ridgeway Avenue, Dunstable	80	Bates	4. 0.0
19.07.67	James Pay 4 Cross Street, Dunstable	78	Bates	3. 0.0
27.08.67	Walter Henry William Quantrell Hall Farm Cottage, Studham	74	Bates	3. 0.0
17.10.67	Rosa Oxenford 13 Woodlands Avenue	77	Bates	3. 0.0
18.01.68	Arthur Pool Hill Top Farm, Studham	58	Bates	3. 0.0
01.02.68	Francis Lawrence Woodward Dunstable	72	Bates	3.10.0
08.02.68	George Pratt 84 Waterlow Road, Dunstable	83	Bates	3.10.0
18.04.68	Elizabeth Ellen Napier Bidwell	93	Bates	5. 0.0
05.05.68	Edith Dorothy Fowler 20 King Street, Dunstable	68	Bates	3.10.0
14.05.68	Violet Chandler Drury Lane	61	Bates	3. 0.0
19.05.68	Ellen Alcock Waterlow Road	88	Bates	3. 0.0
16.12.68	Leonard Charles Sharman	73	Co-op	1. 2.6
01.01.69	William Billington 28 Drury Lane	82	Bates	3.10.0
21.01.69	Robert Mason Rudlin Mountview Avenue, Dunstable	70	Bates	3. 5.0
21.01.69	Frederick George Bodsworth 6 Park Lane, Eaton Bray	73	Bates	4. 0.0
20.03.69	Alan George Emmerson 73 Sundon Road	10	Bates	3.10.0
06.04.69	Albert Glyndwr James 53 Waterlow Road, Dunstable	58	Bates	3. 0.0
09.05.69	Sarak Fensome Studham	89	Bates	3.10.0

Date	Name / Address	Age		Cost
25.05.69	Gwendoline Muriel Laing 18 West Parade		Bates	3. 0.0
27.05.69	Amy Fitzgerald 205 Luton Road, Dunstable	83	Bates	3. 0.0
03.08.69	Rose Irene Loft 15 Woodlands Avenue	54	Neville	5. 0.0
01.09.69	Elizabeth Ralley 40 Marina Drive	88	Bates	3.10.0
19.12.69	Benjamin Charles Houghton Churchfield Road	75	Bates	3. 0.0
27.12.69	Hilda Room 17 Capron Road, Dunstable	72	Bates	3. 0.0
28.12.69	Leslie Robert Bull 19 Church Lane, Eaton Bray	65	Bates	3. 0.0
28.12.69	Gladys Winifred Mather 72 Canesworth Road, Dunstable	49	Bates	3. 6.0
25.05.70	Mary Tearle 38 Totternhoe Road, Eaton Bray	84	Bates	4. 0.0
70	Nellie Tompkins 56 High Street	92	Bates	4. 0.0
13.08.70	Doris Sophia Smith 901 Dunstable Road, Luton	70	Bates	3. 0.0
16.08.70	Horace Alec Tompkins The Limes, Cumberland Street	71	Bates	14 .0.0
14.10.70	Sidney George Smith	76		free
05.01.71	Percy Arthur Mead 110 Manor Par	62	Bates	3.10.0
08.03.71	George Henry Stripp 10 Bedford Road	83	Bates	4. 0.0
29.03.71	Rhoda May Pemberton 30 Cemetery Road	69	Bates	5. 0.0
25.08.71	George Ashdown 41 St Michaels Avenue	87	Bates	4. 0.0
.12.71	Millicent Creamer 54 Chapel Close, Toddington	80	Bates	3. 0.0

				£ p
09.02.72	Ronald Haydon Rodell 1 Whitehouse Close	60	Bates	5.20
16.03.72	Edith May Stearn Primrose Cottage, Queen Street	75	Bates	7.00
04.05.72	Daisy Gadsden 1 Greenways, Eaton Bray	77	Bates	5.20
.72	Annie Tring 52 Princess Street, Dunstable	83	Bates	5.20

The above record shows a total of 231 people prepared by Maud for their final rest, with ages ranging from 9 months to 95. She herself was only 26 when she did her first 'laying out' and it was fifty years later when the final entry was made in her little record book. Her 'customers' included her own two sisters and a number of cousins and other relatives. Her charge for laying out often included an additional charge for 'doing' the funeral tea. Her fees frequently varied to reflect the family's ability to pay and very often she would take part-payment or a tip in the form of a little ornament or other memento from the house. As she used to put it 'just something for me to remember them by'.

APPENDIX 2

CHURCHFIELDS ALLOTMENT HOLDERS

The following is the list of occupiers of allotments at the time of the Luton Rural District Council (Houghton Regis Town Development) Compulsory Purchase Order 1956 as detailed in that Order:

J Baker	C Swile	H G Piper
R A Bliss	G Evans	R C Rawson
R H Bonner	R G Eason	F J Read
V Bozier	N F Richardson	H Stearn
A Bright	F G Foster	G H Stripp
Miss F Bright	E Flecknell	B R Stripp
L C Bright	W Gadsden	W C Richards
A C Bates	A Gadsden	S G Smith
C Malcolm	**G Germaine**	R Stoten
P Tulley	J W Griffin	W Tompkins
Mrs B M Buckingham	J Gosbell	E H Wraight
F Bright	M J S Holwill	R B Wood
H Bandy	R A Henderson	T Wilson
A J Cherry	S Harvey	S Wright
S Clark	H Joyce	A Wrench
F A Calcott	H Giltrow	A H Watts
B F Calcott	R Lithgo	L F Yirrell

231

G Coles

H Cumberland

D L Cross

H Chandler

F Dumpleton

E J Loft

H J Miller

M N Owen

E W Puddefoot

W D Austin

F Morris

G W Eames

S Higgs

H J Prentice

J C H Holloway

APPENDIX 3

COMPULSORY PURCHASE ORDER LAND 1957

The following land was included in the Luton Rural District Council (Houghton Regis Town Development) Compulsory Purchase Order 1956:

ACREAGE	OS Number	OWNER	OCCUPIER
Confirmed at Public Inquiry 1957:			
6.157	301	E G Smith	E G Smith
12.264	302	R O Andrews	R O Andrews
12.85	303	R O Andrews	R O Andrews
14.74	303	R O Andrews	R O Andrews
6.883	352	Vicar of Houghton Regis	Ward Brothers
18.41	354	Vicar of Houghton Regis	Ward Brothers
0.490	304	R O Andrews	R O Andrews
12.254	248	Vicar of Houghton Regis	Allotment Holders as listed (App.2)
5.692	249	E G Smith	E G Smith
2.467	251	E G Smith	E G Smith
22.816	264	E G Smith	E G Smith
15.666	301	E G Smith	E G Smith
4.726	302	R O Andrews	R O Andrews

1.548	262	Mrs S Catling	Mrs S Catling
2.693	261	Mrs S Catling	Mrs S Catling
1.271	260	Mrs L Markall	
0.599	303	R O Andrews	R O Andrews
0.060	304	R O Andrews	R O Andrews
1.010	305	Whitehead Foundation	Mrs S Catling
5.474	307	R O Andrews	R O Andrews
4.303	308	R O Andrews	R O Andrews
0.056	309	R O Andrews	R O Andrews
0.430	303	R O Andrews	R O Andrews
9.076	304	R O Andrews	R O Andrews
1.335	305	Whitehead Foundation	Mrs S Catling
11.66	346	R O Andrews	R O Andrews
1.592	307	R O Andrews	R O Andrews
3.66	339	R O Andrews	R O Andrews
4.795	308	R O Andrews	R O Andrews
4.674	342	R O Andrews	R O Andrews
3.06	309	R O Andrews	R O Andrews

Excluded at Public Inquiry 1957:

2.14	216	Vicar of Houghton Regis	
2.370	252	H T Birchley	H T Birchley
0.492	306	**G W Jackson**	**G W Jackson**
0.008	306	**G W Jackson**	**G W Jackson**

APPENDIX 4

PARISH COUNCIL 1960

The Houghton Regis Parish Council following the May 1960 election was as follows:

Arthur James Cherry, 25 Park Avenue
Sidney Charles Clarke #, 36 Woodlands Avenue
Thomas Clarke, 31 Drury Lane
Thurza Elizabeth Day, 8 Mill Road
Cyril George Dodgson, 20 St Michael's Avenue
Stanley Jack Field, 7 Park Avenue
Frederick John Greer, The Red House, The Green
Stanley Alec Higgs, 9 Bidwell Hill
Irene Betty May Jackson, The Hyde, Sundon Road
George Edward Nye #, 23 Sundon Road
Ronald James Pemberton, The Laurels, Cumberland Street
Alfred Sidney Pinsent, 16 Drury Lane
Thomas James Strange #, 35 Manor Park
Arthur Thody, The Chantry, Sundon Road
Edward Charles Todd, 32 Drury Lane

\# Also a member of Luton Rural District Council

APPENDIX 5

WHERE ARE WE NOW?

It is possible that some reading this book will have known us in our Houghton Regis days and may wonder what became of us all as a family.

My parents, Betty and George Jackson, moved to Pembrokeshire after Dad's early retirement in 1974. They lived first in the village of St Ishmaels and then moved to Hakin, which is part of the town of Milford Haven. They enjoyed a long and happy retirement becoming very much part of the local community. Dad died aged 89 in 2000 and Mum died just over two years later. They are both now reunited with my grandmother Maud Humphrey in the cemetery at Dale on the west coast of Pembrokeshire.

My sister Jennifer married Paul Rayner and lived at Yew Street, Houghton Regis. They have six children – Maxine, Helen, Paula, Stuart, Karl and Rachel. After her divorce from Paul, Jennifer moved to Pembrokeshire where she still lives in the small town of Neyland. Jennifer has not enjoyed the best of health but plays an active part in the life of her local community and looks forward to visits from her numerous grand and great-grand children.

My sister Margaret married Phillip Holland and they have two children, Chris and Libby. Maggie worked in the personnel department at AC- Delco and actually produced Dad's retirement certificate. The family lived for a good number of years in Dunstable before moving to the Bristol area when Phil's work with Rolls Royce was transferred there. Maggie worked for several years in what was the DHSS and Phil is still with Rolls Royce. They live a few miles from me in the Staple Hill area of Bristol.

My brother Nigel served an engineering apprenticeship at AC-Delco and made the move to Pembrokeshire when Mum and Dad retired, finding work with an engineering company in Milford Haven, which about ten years later re-located to Yate in South Gloucestershire. Nigel married Janice Roberts who had two children Karen and Evan from her previous marriage. Nigel is now a senior engineer with a company specialising in pumps, turbines and equipment for the water treatment industry and he and Janice live just around the corner from me in Thornbury, South Gloucestershire.

I married Haidee Coupe from Wrestlingworth in 1962 and we have two sons, Bill and Douglas. When I left the Meteorological Office I became a Police Officer serving in Huntingdonshire (later Mid-Anglia and now Cambridgeshire) and then in the Pembrokeshire Division of the Dyfed Powys Constabulary. After a brief period with the Dyfed Rural Council where I worked with the Herald Bard of Wales, we took a village pub, the Brook Inn at St Ishmaels in Pembrokeshire where we stayed for six years. Before the end of this period I had also become Town Clerk and Financial Officer in Pembroke. In 1984 I became Town Clerk at Thornbury in South Gloucestershire, taking early retirement from this post in 2001. Haidee had previously taken early retirement from Clerical Medical Insurance in Bristol and we have both pursued various interests part-time since. Haidee is a qualified massage therapist and was also a receptionist at the local golf club, and most recently I have served as President of the Hearts of Oak Friendly Society.

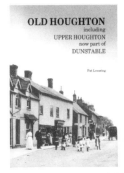
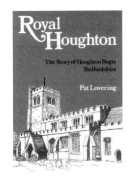

OLD HOUGHTON
including Upper Houghton now part of Dunstable
Pat Lovering

More than 170 photographs of village life in historic Houghton Regis, Bedfordshire, taken over the last 100 years and acquired from both private and public sources are included in this publication. Because of subsequent boundary changes many early photographs cover parts of modern Dunstable.

The author Pat Lovering, is a local private tutor who has lived and worked in Houghton Regis and Dunstable for some years. She became interested in assembling this collection of photographs when compiling her other book "Royal Houghton".

ROYAL HOUGHTON
The Story of Houghton Regis Bedfordshire
Pat Lovering

People still find parish churches a fascination, so that week by week visitors to our church for weddings and baptisms especially stop to ask questions. How old is the church? Where did Regis come from? These and many other questions are the beginning of the fascinating trail taking us back nearly one thousand years.

Did you know that Houghton Regis was a Royal Manor in Saxon times? It also appeared in the Doomsday Book of 1086. Henry 1st gave land from his manor of Houghton Regis to make the new town of Dunstable.

All these facts and many other details of Houghton Regis from earliest times to present day are included in this book.

DUNSTABLE SCHOOL
1888-1971
F.M. Bancroft

"It was not one of the leading schools in the country...But it was a grammar school, a good grammar school, and it gave a sound all round education aligned with sporting activities of note. It taught courtesy, politeness and the home truths of life. And because of the masters over the years and a lot of the boys who went there it was a character school, with a happy atmosphere."

So, for all these reasons along with their own personal memories, though the school was superseded over a generation ago thousands of Old Boys still remember it with deep affection and gratitude.

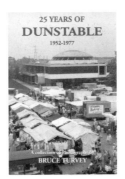

25 YEARS OF DUNSTABLE 1952-1977
A collection of photographs
Bruce Turvey

An era of enormous change in the town, 1952-1977, is commemorated in this superb collection of over 400 photographs – the best from Bruce Turvey's professional collection of over 100,000. Originally published to mark the Queen's Silver Jubilee, her Golden Jubilee seems a fitting moment for its re-issue.

Changes include the disappearance of key old landmarks such as the Town Hall, the Red Lion and the California swimming pool, as well as the opening of the prestigious Civic (Queensway) Hall, the circular Catholic Church and the Quadrant Shopping Centre. Here are glimpses of other outstanding occasions, including Whipsnade's 21st Birthday party, the Pageant depicting 750 years of town history, and the granting of the Freedom of the Borough to the Herts and Beds Yeomanry – six years before the town's loss of that status in 1974.

Famous visitors abound – four Prime Ministers, along with personalities like Kenneth More, Arthur Askey, David Kossoff, Brenda Lee, George Best, Mary Peters, Hugh Gaitskell and the Duchess of Gloucester. And of course there are hundreds of local people pictured in the photographs of sports teams, coach outings, dinner dances, carnival floats, retirement parties and uniformed organisations.

The book opens with a snow scene and closes with a heat wave. In between are the myriad events that comprise the life of a market town during three different decades a generation ago.

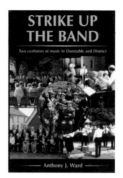

STRIKE UP THE BAND

Two centuries of music in Dunstable and District

Anthony J. Ward

In 'Strike Up The Band', the Author traces the history of music making in Dunstable and District from the earliest times where information is available, up to the present day. It is derived from a wider ongoing project by the author. The book particularly emphasises the history and development of Brass Bands, Orchestras and other groups, recording their contributions to the changing life of the Town and District over the centuries, and highlighting the various celebrations that have taken place over so many years. The book closes with a series of chapters on the three local Senior Schools in Dunstable with their bands, orchestras and music.

The design of the book is largely based on a collection of photographs and memorabilia, derived from the wide number of contributors having connections with the organisations featured in the book, featuring their recollections of events and personalities. The story of music making in Dunstable and its surrounding areas is shown in the context of the history of the area and its citizens.

The Book Castle